Endorsements

"Dr. John MacArthur has been faithfully explaining and proclaiming God's Word for years. With this book, *None Other,* he expounds the character of God with clarity, passion, warmth, and urgency. In a time of theological confusion, Dr. MacArthur upholds Scripture and speaks clearly to the church and to the world about who our Lord is. I am grateful to Dr. MacArthur for his service, and I commend this book whole-heartedly. It is a gift to the people of God."

—Dr. R.C. Sproul
Founder and Chairman, Ligonier Ministries
Sanford, Fla.

"For over four decades, John MacArthur has faithfully exposited God's Word and has taught a generation of Christians to value sound doctrine and fidelity to the Word of God. At the heart of that teaching and preaching ministry has been a robust commitment to the Bible's teaching on the character of God. This brief biblical and theological exploration of God's attributes is rich both in theology and devotion. This book is a welcome resource for any Christian who seeks to know and to love our triune, sovereign God as He has revealed himself in Scripture."

—R. Albert Mohler Jr.
President, The Southern Baptist Theological Seminary
Louisville, Ky.

"Rich fare indeed, and most welcome from one of today's most beloved and trusted expositors, addressing our greatest need—knowing God. With the skill of a master theologian and the heart of a tender shepherd, Dr. John MacArthur provides the richest of material that will edify, nourish, and grow all who read it. A book to read and re-read, and to give to others with assured confidence that this will do them much good."

—Dr. Derek W.H. Thomas
Senior Minister, First Presbyterian Church
Columbia, S.C.

"In this work, the reader is loving, patiently, and unapologetically confronted with the God of the Bible. Dr. MacArthur makes no attempt to reconcile the testimony of God's Word with the contrary opinions of fallen man. He simply points us to the Scriptures and expounds them without additions or subtractions. In a day of confusion, the reader will find in these pages a trustworthy treatise regarding some of the most important, yet misunderstood, aspects of God's nature. Do not be misled by the brevity of this work. It is chock-full of theological truth set forth with clarity and simplicity. For the new believer, it is a valuable introduction to the God of Scripture. For the seasoned pastor, it is a reminder to hold fast to the biblical view of God and to proclaim Him to the people."

—Rev. Paul Washer
Director, HeartCry Missionary Society
Radford, Va.

NONE
OTHER

NONE OTHER

DISCOVERING THE GOD OF THE BIBLE

JOHN MACARTHUR

$\mathbb{R}$ *Reformation Trust*   A DIVISION OF LIGONIER MINISTRIES, ORLANDO, FL

None Other: Discovering the God of the Bible
© 2017 by John MacArthur

Published by Reformation Trust Publishing
A division of Ligonier Ministries
421 Ligonier Court, Sanford, FL 32771
Ligonier.org   ReformationTrust.com

Printed in York, Pennsylvania
Maple Press
December 2016
First edition

ISBN 978-1-56769-738-4 (Hardcover)
ISBN 978-1-56769-739-1 (ePub)
ISBN 978-1-56769-740-7 (Kindle)

Cover design by Metaleap Creative.
Interior design and typeset: Katherine Lloyd, The DESK

Scripture quotations taken from the New American Standard Bible (NASB), Copyright © 1960, 1962, 1963, 1968, 1971, 1972, 1973, 1975, 1977, 1995 by The Lockman Foundation. Used by permission. www.Lockman.org

Library of Congress Cataloging-in-Publication Data

Names: MacArthur, John, 1939- author.
Title: None other : discovering the God of the Bible / John MacArthur.
Description: First edition. | Orlando, FL : Reformation Trust Publishing, 2017. | Includes bibliographical references and index.
Identifiers: LCCN 2016035766 | ISBN 9781567697384
Subjects: LCSH: God (Christianity)--Attributes.
Classification: LCC BT130 .M325 2017 | DDC 231/.4--dc23
LC record available at https://lccn.loc.gov/2016035766

CONTENTS

Chapter One

THE GOD OF THE BIBLE IS GRACIOUS

Knowing *about* God is not the same as knowing God. Almost anyone can tell you something about the Lord— the facts about Him are not a secret. He is merciful and kind. He loves sinners in spite of their sin. He's the Creator and sustainer of the universe, and He is the rightful "Judge of all" (Heb. 12:23). But those facts represent only a few facets of who God truly is. And for those who do not know and love Him, they offer little more than a veiled glimpse of His nature.

In these pages, we want to get beyond the mere facts of who God is and develop an understanding of His character. We want to know His heart and His will and delve deeply into His complicated relationship with humanity. In simple terms, we don't merely want to know about God, we want to know *Him*.

When it comes to knowing the nature of God, one of the best places to start—and certainly one of the most important truths about His character and how He relates to us—is His

1

grace. It is fundamental to the nature of God to be gracious. He must manifest that grace, and He will be exalted for it forever.

While the grace of God is most clearly and fully manifest in the sacrifice of His Son and His redemption of sinners, its expression is not isolated to the person and work of Christ. God's grace is older than history, reaching back before the creation of time itself. It is not merely poured out in the moment of salvation; it is evident throughout His eternal plan of redemption. After all, He chose those whom He would save before the foundation of the world (Eph. 1:4).

Theologians refer to this precious truth as the doctrine of election, and it has been a major point of debate and division in the church. The truth about election is essential to understanding who God is, His plan of redemption, and His design for the church. But some who profess love for God and belief in the Bible nevertheless resent and even despise this doctrine. Many people seem to think John Calvin invented the doctrine of election, even though it is clearly a prominent doctrine in Scripture. I once heard a well-known preacher say he believes Calvinism is the single greatest danger to the church today. He went on to make it clear that what actually made him leery was the doctrine of election.

But rejecting this doctrine has major negative implications, especially with regard to the practical aspects of evangelism and Christian ministry. Christians who don't believe God sovereignly draws His elect to Christ are forced by their theological perspective to take a very pragmatic approach to evangelism.

They become more concerned with what "works" than with what's true, because their doctrine leads them to believe everything hinges on their own skill, cleverness, or persuasive abilities. What an enormous burden and responsibility they have taken on themselves!

However, the doctrine of election should not extinguish the church's evangelistic efforts. If anything, it ought to spur us on. While the Lord knows whom He chose in eternity past, we do not have insight into His electing work (cf. Deut. 29:29). Instead, we must fervently pursue every sinner while there is still time to repent. We need to proclaim the blessed truth of Isaiah 59:1–2 faithfully to every ear that will hear: "Behold, the Lord's hand is not so short that it cannot save; nor is His ear so dull that it cannot hear. But your iniquities have made a separation between you and your God, and your sins have hidden His face from you so that He does not hear." That's the responsibility of faith—that as long as we draw breath, we are duty bound to preach the good news of Jesus Christ as winsomely and persuasively as possible, so that others may be led to a saving knowledge of Him. "Knowing the fear of the Lord, we persuade others" (2 Cor. 5:11).

Moreover, we need to hold the doctrine of election with great humility. Our salvation is not a credit to us but an unearned gift from a gracious God. And He has left us in this world for the time being to extend that gift to others through the proclamation of His Word.

Understanding God's sovereign grace is at the heart of what the church is and how it functions. A right view of God's grace informs how we relate to other believers. It informs how we evangelize the lost. It defines a pastor's role. It touches every aspect of life in the body of Christ.[1]

Grace and Justice

The typical complaint of those who are skeptical about the doctrine of election (or even opposed to it) is that it makes God seem unfair. And that may indeed seem to be the case—if you measure what's "fair" by fallen human judgment. *Why doesn't God treat everyone the same?* we think. *That's what I would do.* But God doesn't think the way we think or do what we would do. "'My thoughts are not your thoughts, nor are your ways My ways,' declares the Lord" (Isa. 55:8). He is wiser and more just than we are. He is not to be measured by any human standard. Remember the words of the Apostle Paul, who said, "Oh, the depth of the riches both of the wisdom and knowledge of God!" He goes on to say, "How unsearchable are His judgments and unfathomable His ways!" (Rom. 11:33).

Furthermore, the question we should ask when we ponder the doctrine of election is not "Why doesn't God save everyone?" but "Why does God save anyone at all?" He's certainly not obligated to show mercy. That's what makes grace gracious.

When considering what's fair in the matter of election, all human presumptions and standards must be set aside. Instead, the nature of God must be the focus. This leads us to ask, what is divine justice? Simply stated, it is an essential attribute of God whereby He, infinitely and in perfect justice, does what

He wants. As William Perkins said, "We must not think that God doeth a thing because it is good and right, but rather is the thing good and right because God willeth and worketh it."[2] God defines justice. He Himself is by nature just and righteous, and whatever He does reflects His nature. So whatever He does is right. His own free will (and nothing else) is what determines justice, for whatever He wills is just; and it is just because He wills it, not vice versa. There is no higher standard of righteousness than God Himself.

In Luke 4, a brief incident occurred that had tremendous impact. Jesus was speaking in the synagogue in Nazareth. He was handed the scroll of Scripture, and He turned to the next regular reading from Isaiah. Luke 4:18–19 says He read, "The Spirit of the Lord is upon Me, Because He anointed Me to preach the gospel to the poor. He has sent Me to proclaim release to the captives, and recovery of sight to the blind, to set free those who are oppressed, to proclaim the favorable year of the Lord."

Then He closed the book, gave it back to the attendant, and sat down. The eyes of all in the synagogue were fixed upon Him. And He said to them, "Today this Scripture has been fulfilled in your hearing" (v. 21). In other words, the One the prophet said would come to preach had come.

Then Luke records, "And all were speaking well of Him, and wondering at the gracious words which were falling from His lips; and they were saying, 'Is this not Joseph's son?'" (v. 22). They knew Joseph. But they didn't know anything about Joseph that could cause his Son to be as special as this man seemed to be.

And then He said to them, "No doubt you will quote this proverb to Me, 'Physician, heal yourself! Whatever we heard was done at Capernaum, do here in your hometown as well'" (v. 23). Christ knew that they would want to see some proof that He was who He claimed to be—some miraculous manifestation of His power. Then He said:

> Truly I say to you, no prophet is welcome in his hometown. But I say to you in truth, there were many widows in Israel in the days of Elijah, when the sky was shut up for three years and six months, when a great famine came over all the land; and yet Elijah was sent to none of them, but only to Zarephath, in the land of Sidon, to a woman who was a widow. And there were many lepers in Israel in the time of Elisha the prophet; and none of them was cleansed, but only Naaman the Syrian. (vv. 24–27)

What kind of an answer is that? What was He saying to them? His point was simple: God has not ordained that everyone be healed. Furthermore, God Himself has determined which widow gets healed and which leper gets healed. It doesn't hinge on human free will. Even Christ's miracles would be done according to the sovereign will of God, not in answer to the demands of people in Jesus' own hometown. He was saying, in effect, "You may expect me to do in this town what was done in Capernaum, but God doesn't work that way. God sovereignly chooses what He will do."

Then, verse 28 records the first New Testament reaction to the doctrine of election: "And all the people in the synagogue were filled with rage."

The real question was, would they tolerate the truth that God's grace is subject only to the counsel of His own will? Would they tolerate God's sovereign election? Even respectable worshipers in Jesus' hometown synagogue hated this truth.

In Revelation 19:6, we're told, "The Lord our God, the Almighty, reigns." Both in heaven and on earth, He is the controller and disposer of all creatures. He is the Most High, and "all the inhabitants of the earth are accounted as nothing, but He does according to His will in the host of heaven and among the inhabitants of earth; and no one can ward off His hand or say to Him, 'What have You done?'" (Dan. 4:35). He is the Almighty who works all things out according to the counsel of His will. He is the heavenly Potter who takes good-for-nothing sinners and shapes them into useful vessels. Scripture pictures the fallen human race as a lump of clay—a dirty, formless material that, left to itself, would certainly harden into something utterly worthless and altogether unattractive. From that one common lump of muck, the divine Potter forms unique objects for various purposes. Like an earthly potter who makes both ashtrays and fancy serving dishes, the heavenly Potter fashions vessels for honor as well as dishonor (Rom. 9:21)—some to show His grace and glory; others to serve as vessels of His wrath. Every expression of His righteous character—including His utter hatred of sin—is thus put on display in accord with His sovereign will. And Scripture furthermore says He always accomplishes His perfect design with patience and kindness, never with malice or ill will: "What if God, desiring to show his wrath and to make known his power, has endured with much patience vessels of wrath prepared for destruction, in order to make known the riches of his glory for vessels of mercy, which he has prepared beforehand for glory?" (vv. 22–23).

Ultimately, then, God is the One who decides and determines every man's destiny. As our Creator and rightful Ruler, He carefully governs each detail in His universe—which is another way of saying He is God, the sovereign and almighty Lord.

Frankly, the only reason to believe in election is because it is found explicitly in God's Word. No man, and no committee of men, originated this doctrine. It's like the doctrine of eternal punishment: it conflicts with all the natural inclinations and preferences of the carnal human mind. It's repugnant to the sentiments of the unregenerate heart. And—like the doctrine of the Holy Trinity and the miraculous birth of our Savior— the truth of election, because it has been revealed by God, must be embraced with simple, solemn, settled faith. If you have a Bible and you believe what it says, you have no choice.

Even the *foreknowledge* referred to in 1 Peter 1:20 is not to be confused with *foresight*. Mere foresight on God's part would make man both sovereign and praiseworthy, deserving of credit for making a good choice by seeking God and choosing to believe in Him. Such teaching is an assault on God's sovereignty, making the Lord merely a reactor, waiting in heaven and hoping people will repent by their own free-will choice. God's foreknowledge, according to this view, is little more than the ability to peer into the future and observe what His creatures will do.

But 1 Peter 1:20 says of Christ that "He was foreknown before the foundation of the world" as the Lamb of God, unblemished and spotless, who would shed His blood as the price of His people's redemption. That's not talking about something God foresaw as a passive observer. It's describing the plan of salvation, which He sovereignly ordained before the foundation of the world.

As we think about the justice of God as being representative of His character and not subject to fallen assumptions, we begin to understand that God—in the nature of His own sovereignty—defines everything that He does not only as just, but also as perfect. The Creator owes nothing to the creature, not even that which He is graciously pleased to give. So God does exactly what God chooses to do. Nothing can thwart His will or overpower Him. That's actually the very essence of what we are confessing when we acknowledge Him as Almighty God.

God's Freedom to Elect

So God does whatever He wants. Everything He does is true and right *because He does it.* He would never do anything that's inconsistent with His own holy character. He Himself is therefore the standard of what is holy and righteous. In other words, He embodies all that is truly holy.

That's what we mean when we say God is holy. It is a principle that underlies everything Scripture teaches. It is certainly one of the fundamental precepts on which the doctrine of election is grounded.

Furthermore, the choosing of people for salvation cannot be isolated from every other thing God has chosen to do, because in the big picture, God has ordained everything that comes to pass. Everything that God does He chooses to do, and His choices are free from any influence outside Himself. Therefore, the doctrine of election fits into this fuller comprehension of a sovereign God. That is election in its broadest sense, and it is evident on nearly every page of Scripture.

In the very act of creation, God created exactly what He wanted to create in exactly the way He wanted to create it, allowing for the very things that occurred in human history in order that He might accomplish the redemptive plan He had already designed. He chose a nation, Israel, not because they were better than any other people or because they were more desirable than any other people, but simply because He chose them. Moses told Israel, "The Lord your God has chosen you to be a people for His own possession out of all the peoples who are on the face of the earth. The Lord did not set His love on you nor choose you because you were more in number than any of the peoples, for you were the fewest of all peoples, but because the Lord loved you" (Deut. 7:6a–8b). Like all the elect, Israel was "predestined according to His purpose who works all things after the counsel of His will" (Eph. 1:11).

In Psalm 105:43, He calls Israel "His chosen ones." Psalm

135:4 says, "The Lord has chosen Jacob for Himself." In Deuteronomy 7 and again in Deuteronomy 14, we find these words: "The Lord your God has chosen you to be a people for His own possession out of all the peoples who are on the face of the earth." Scripture doesn't attempt to defend or explain the choice—it simply asserts that God did the choosing.

In the same way, God has sovereignly chosen from the very beginning everything that fits into His master plan of redemption. From its opening verses, the New Testament is replete with examples of God's sovereignty at work. He elected His Son as Redeemer and appointed the time and means of His arrival on earth. It should be no surprise that He even chose the elect body who would be His Son's bride—the church.

His glorious plan for each individual Christian is likewise consistent with the way He has always operated—sovereignly. He has not handed His sovereignty over to something as vacillating and arbitrary as human free will. Christ told His disciples, "You did not choose Me but I chose you, and appointed you that you would go and bear fruit, and that your fruit would remain" (John 15:16). The Apostle Paul says even the good works we do as believers were prepared by God "beforehand" (Eph. 2:10).

Christians from the very outset have understood this. In Acts 13:48, Luke says, "As many as had been appointed to eternal life believed." And, of course, the ninth chapter of Romans contains a monumental passage on the elective purposes of God as manifested in the choices of Jacob and Esau, and how God chose whom He chose—not on the basis of anything they had done, but according to His own sovereign, free, and uninfluenced purpose. "Does not the potter have a right over the clay?" (Rom. 9:21) and "Who are you, O man, who answers back to God? The thing molded will not say to the molder, 'Why did you make me like this,' will it?" (v. 20). We're better off to keep silent than to question God's sovereign purposes.

Election and the Church

Throughout the New Testament, there are references to the church as the elect—chosen by God. Ephesians 1 says we were chosen in Him, by His love, before the foundation of the world, that we might be brought to faith in Christ. In 1 Thessalonians, Paul addresses the congregation as "brethren beloved by God," and told them, "[we know] His choice of you" (1:4). In 2 Thessalonians 2:13, we read, "But we should always give thanks to God for you, brethren beloved by the Lord, because God has chosen you from the beginning for salvation through sanctification by the Spirit and faith in the truth." It doesn't get any clearer than that: God has chosen you from the beginning for salvation.

In Matthew 16:18, Jesus said, "I will build My church; and the gates of Hades will not overpower it." This is a monumental statement: "*I* will build My church." "I *will* build My church." It's a statement of certainty, and of intimacy—"*My* church." It's also a statement of invincibility—God's church will stand against the gates of Hades, which is a Jewish euphemism for death. The implication here is important: if Hades is the abode of the dead, you get in by dying, so it's simply a reference to death, which is Satan's greatest weapon. Jesus was saying, "I will build My church—and the worst that can be done to stop it, the death of My people, will not overpower it."

This is a very straightforward promise. The immutable, sovereign, faithful, gracious, omnipotent Lord of heaven—whose Word can never return void but always accomplishes the purpose to which He sends it; whose plans always come to pass; whose will is ultimately fulfilled; whose plan is in the end invincible—He has spoken and said, "I will build My church." Nothing can prevent that.

That's the end result of God's work in election. In the first chapter of Titus, Paul gives us some insight into how the plan of redemption started. We often skim quickly over the introductory parts of Paul's epistles, but they are usually pregnant with meaning—and in this case profoundly so. In Titus 1, Paul describes his work as "a bond-servant of God," dividing his ministry into three categories of God's saving work.

First, it unfolded "for the faith of those chosen of God" (v. 1). This referred to the evangelistic emphasis of his ministry, the matter of justification being the initial objective. Paul was commissioned by God to bring the message of the gospel in order that "those chosen of God" might be redeemed. In effect, he was saying, "I preach the gospel so that the elect can hear it and believe." That emphasis in Paul's ministry stressed the doctrine of *justification*—how sinners can gain a right standing before God.

Second, there was an emphasis on *sanctification*—he brought "the knowledge of the truth which is according to godliness" (v. 1). There is evangelism and then there is a ministry of edification. Paul brought the gospel to the elect so they can hear and believe; and he brought the truth of God to those who believe so that they can move toward godliness.

Paul also emphasized the "hope of eternal life" (v. 2), and therein lies the third emphasis in his ministry: *glorification,* which brings about immense encouragement in the face of difficulty in this life.

Those are the three dimensions of salvation—justification, sanctification, and glorification. This was the salvific character of Paul's ministry. As an Apostle of Jesus Christ, he brought the whole counsel of God: God's justifying work, His sanctifying work, and His glorifying work.

So Paul proclaimed the gospel of Christ with great clarity to those who heard him, so that the elect would hear and believe. Then, to those who believed, he taught the truth so they could grow in grace and in the knowledge of Christ. Then he showed them what was to come in the hope of eternal life, which gave them great encouragement in the midst of difficulty. He emphasized those three familiar things—justification, through which we have been saved from the *penalty* of sin; sanctification, in which we are being saved from the *power* of sin; and glorification, by which we will one day be saved from the *presence* of sin. That is the fullness of salvation, past, present, and future. The heart and soul of Paul's ministry was the task of proclaiming all three dimensions of gospel truth.

But notice the end of verse 2, which is the key: this whole unfolding miracle of salvation comes from God, "who cannot lie," and, as it says at the end of verse 2, "promised [it] long ages ago."

"Long ages ago" is a biblical expression referring to eternity past—the age before time began (cf. Acts 15:18; Rom. 16:25). It is equivalent to the expression "before the foundation of the world" (John 17:24; Matt. 25:34; 1 Peter 1:20). So Paul is saying God decreed the plan of redemption and promised salvation before the beginning of time.

"Promised"—to whom? Not to any human being, because none of us had been created. And not to the angels, because there is no redemption for angels. Second Timothy 1:8–9 helps answer the question. There, it says, "Therefore do not be ashamed of the testimony of our Lord or of me His prisoner, but join with me in suffering for the gospel according to the power of God, who has saved us and called us with a holy calling, not according to our works, but according to His own purpose and grace which was *granted us in Christ Jesus from all eternity*" (emphasis added). To whom did God make this promise? It's an intra-Trinitarian promise; a promise from the Father to the Son.

This is sacred ground, and our best understanding of it is still feeble, so we must tread carefully. We recognize that there is an intra-Trinitarian love between Father and Son, the likes of which is incomprehensible and inscrutable to us (John 3:35; 17:26).

But this we know about love: it gives. And at some eternal moment, the Father desired to express His perfect love for the Son, and the way He determined to do so was to give to the Son a redeemed humanity—whose purpose would be, throughout all of the eons of eternity, to praise and glorify the Son and serve Him perfectly. That was the Father's love gift.

The Father wanted to give this gift to the Son, and He predetermined to do it. Not only that, but He predetermined who would make up that redeemed humanity, and wrote their names down in a book of life before the world began. He set them aside for the purpose of praising and glorifying the name of Christ forever.

That means, in a sense, that you and I are somewhat incidental to the real issue here. *Salvation is primarily for the honor of the Son, not the honor of the sinner.* The purpose of the Father's love gift is not to save you so you can have a happy life; it is to save you so that you can spend eternity praising the Son.

An Eternal Expression of Love

John's gospel gives us remarkable insight into this very theme. In John 6:37, Jesus said, "All that the Father *gives Me* will come to Me, and the one who comes to Me I will certainly not cast out" (emphasis added). Every redeemed individual is a part of an elect body chosen from humanity in order to be given as a gift of love from the Father to the Son. This is not a matter of contingency. Jesus said, "All that the Father gives Me *will* come to me."

Jesus further says, "No one can come to Me unless the Father who sent Me draws him" (v. 44). All whom the Father gives are drawn; all who are drawn come; all who come will be received; and He will never cast any of them out. Why would the Son reject a love gift from the Father? Our salvation in Christ is secure not because believers are so inherently desirable—we're not. We're secure because we are a gift from the Father to the Son, and because of the love of the Son for the Father. Christ responds to the Father's expression of love in perfect gratitude, opening His arms to embrace the gift. The same infinite, inscrutable love that set us aside as a gift in eternity past now holds us secure in loving gratitude forever.

There's more here. In verse 39, we read, "This is the will of Him who sent Me, that of all that He has given Me I lose nothing, but raise it up on the last day." Apparently, this is how it worked: the Father chose all of those who would be redeemed, who are to be given to the Son as an expression of love. He wrote down their names in the Lamb's Book of Life. Then, in time, the Father draws them. When the Father draws them, the sinners come; when they come, the Son receives them. When He receives them, He keeps them and raises them up on the last day to bring the plan to fruition. He *must* do this, according to verse 38: "For I have come down from heaven, not to do My own will, but the will of Him who sent Me." And this is the will of the One who sent Jesus: that of all whom the Father has given Him, He loses none, but raises each one up on the last day.

Inherent in this doctrine, then, is the security of the believer—better known as the perseverance of the saints. It is all built into the plan. Consider the incident in John 18, when the soldiers came to take Jesus into captivity in the garden of Gethsemane. Twice Jesus said, "Whom do you seek?"

(John 18:4, 7). They responded, "Jesus the Nazarene" (vv. 5, 7). Then He said to them, referring to the disciples, "Let these go their way" (v. 8). Why did He want the disciples to escape arrest? John explained that it was in order "to fulfill the word which He spoke, 'Of those whom You have given Me I lost not one'" (v. 9).

Hypothetically, if Jesus had allowed them to be arrested, their faith wouldn't have survived the test—so He didn't let it happen. That's how He holds His own: it's not just because He said it. It's because He *does* it. He has lost none of them, and He never will. He'll bring them all the way to resurrection, because they're love gifts from the Father. They're precious—not inherently in who they are, but because they are expressions of the Father's perfect love to Him for the purpose of glorifying, honoring, and serving Him throughout all eternity.

If there is a circumstance that would be more than they could bear, He'll make sure it doesn't happen to them. He "will not allow you to be tempted beyond what you are able, but with the temptation will provide the way of escape also, so that you will be able to endure it" (1 Cor. 10:13). If He has to, He'll providentially intervene. Meanwhile, as He sits at God's right hand, He "intercedes for us" (Rom. 8:34). Hebrews 7:25 points to the security we have through Christ's ongoing work on our behalf: "Therefore He is able also to save forever those who draw near to God through Him, since He always lives to make intercession for them." The perseverance of the saints is guaranteed, not by some detached divine fiat; the success of God's saving work is ensured by the ongoing, personal, attentive care of the Savior, the High Priest, who intercedes for His people to ensure that we are held secure in the plan of redemption.

Consider the High Priestly Prayer in John 17. Jesus was anticipating the cross, realizing that He would suffer the wrath of God against the sins of the world, expressed in those provocative words, "My God, My God, why have You forsaken Me?" (Matt. 27:46). And there were elements of that experience that are infinitely appalling—a horror that cannot be fathomed by the finite human mind. But Jesus wasn't concerned about Himself. He could say on the cross, "Father, into Your hands I commit My spirit" (Luke 23:46). He had no problem in trusting God with Himself. Looking ahead to the terror of the cross in John 17, He prayed not for *Himself,* but for *His own.* He had the responsibility to hold on to them, losing none, and to raise them up at the last day. And even when He was on the verge of giving His very life for them, His concern was not about His own suffering; it was about what might happen to His people in an interval in which He would not be in a position to care for them.

So he prayed for them. "Now they have come to know that everything You have given Me is from You; for the words which You gave Me I have given to them; and they received them and truly understood that I came forth from You, and they believed that You sent Me. I ask on their behalf; I do not ask on behalf of the world, but of those whom You have given Me; for they are Yours" (John 17:7–9). He was saying: *They are Yours, You gave them to Me, and I'm not going to lose them—but I'm going to go through something here and I don't know what's going to happen to them when I'm not there to hold them, even if just for a moment.*

He continued: "I am no longer in the world; and yet they themselves are in the world, and I come to You. Holy Father, keep them in Your name" (v. 11). That's the main request of the whole chapter—"keep them in Your name." It's an incredible request: *Father, I can't hold them for this time when your wrath will be poured out on Me; would You just take over for Me and keep them? I have been faithful to hold them—but there's going to be a moment when I can't hold them. Would You do it then?* Then, continuing in the next verse: "While I was with them, I was keeping them in Your name which You have given Me; and I guarded them and not one of them perished but the son of perdition, so that the Scripture would be fulfilled" (v. 12). He said, *I've been keeping them just as I said I would. Now I just need you to keep them for the time when I'm suffering on their behalf.*

Why did the Father give them to the Son? Toward the end of His prayer, Jesus reaffirmed why: "for You loved Me before the foundation of the world" (v. 24). This is the key—the Father's perfect love for the Son.

The truth of God's sovereign election is high doctrine—far beyond our ability to comprehend completely. It is, after all, dealing with intra-Trinitarian expressions of love that are ultimately unfathomable. And yet, it is a glorious and uplifting, soul-satisfying truth, if we faithfully embrace what Scripture reveals about it.

Election and Christlikeness

From heaven's perspective, the ultimate end of election, the ultimate purpose behind God's grace poured out on us, is the eternal glorification of the Son. But to understand God's individual purpose in electing His people for salvation, we need to consider Romans 8:29: "For those whom He foreknew, He also predestined to become conformed to the image of His Son, so that He would be the firstborn among many brethren."

Two things stand out among the many points that could be addressed in that verse. First, we were predestined *to be conformed to the image of God's own Son.* God's elective purpose is not merely about the beginning of our salvation—He predestined us to the absolute perfection we will (by His grace) enjoy at the end of the process. Paul didn't say, "He predestined them to be justified," but, "He also predestined them to *become* conformed to the image of His Son." When will that happen? It's happening now, if you are a believer, even if the progress seems so slow as to be imperceptible. And it will be brought to instantaneous completion "when He appears" (1 John 3:2). That is a reference to the second coming, when the bodies of the saints are resurrected and glorified. Thus redemption will be complete. The verse goes on to say, "we will be like Him, because we will see Him just as He is." That's what Romans 8:19 refers to as "the revealing of the sons of God." And Christ then becomes the chief One among many who are made like Him.

As much as glorified humanity can be like incarnate deity,

we'll be like Christ, and He will not be ashamed to call us brothers. Paul said, "I press on toward the goal for the prize of the upward call of God in Christ Jesus" (Phil. 3:14). What's the prize of the upward call? Christlikeness. If someone is saved in order to be like Christ in glory, then his goal here is as much as possible—by the power of the Spirit—to be like Him *now*. That's the goal all believers must press toward. We will be made like Christ, conformed to the image of the Son, and He will be the chief one among us all. This is the elective purpose of God. And no one's going to fall through the cracks. His perfect plan will come to pass, without fail.

There's a remarkable conclusion to this in 1 Corinthians 15:24–28. A time is coming when the last enemy—death—will be abolished; when Christ, the King of the universe, will take His rightful throne and reign supreme because all enemies will be in subjection under His feet. All redeemed humanity will be gathered into glory and made like Jesus Christ. When all of that is done—"When all things are subjected to Him, then the Son Himself also will be subjected to the One who subjected all things to Him, so that God may be all in all" (v. 28).

That verse does not mean Christ takes a place of subordination or inferiority to the Father, but just the opposite. What that text suggests is that when the love gift of redeemed humanity has been given to Jesus Christ, He will take them and give it, *along with Himself,* back to the Father as a reciprocal expression of the same infinite love. Then (without divesting Himself of His humanity or His role as our great High Priest), He takes His former place in the Godhead, to reign in His former, full, and glorious place at the Father's right hand—"so that God may be all in all."

Thus the doctrine of election cannot be taken as if it was an insignificant idea or isolated as fodder for debate. It encompasses the whole of redemptive history.

Christ's Role in the Grace of God

There's one remaining component to address: the role that Jesus played. There had to come a point where the Father said to the Son, "In order to make this happen, You must go into the world and be the offering for their sins." When Jesus said in John 6:38 that He came into the world to do the Father's will, He meant that He had come to die. This is how precious the church is: it's the Lord's gift from the Father to the Son, but He had to sacrifice His Son to obtain it.

It is also precious because of what it cost the Son to receive this gift. In 2 Corinthians 8:9, we read, "For you know the grace of our Lord Jesus Christ, that though He was rich, yet for your sake He became poor, so that you through His poverty might become rich." How rich is God? Boundlessly, infinitely rich. Jesus was rich spiritually with the riches of God, and yet He did something in order that *you* might become spiritually rich with the riches of God: He became poor.

Many theologians and commentators agree that, in this verse, Paul is giving a description of Jesus' earthly financial condition—His earthly poverty and economic deprivation. But I would suggest that the Son's earthly economic status is insignificant in terms of His redemptive work. The poverty spoken of here is not earthly economics; it is a divestiture of the prerogatives of His deity.

That poverty is defined in Philippians 2:6–8: "Although He [Christ] existed in the form of God, did not regard equality with God a thing to be grasped, but emptied Himself, taking the form of a bond-servant, and being made in the likeness of men. Being found in appearance as a man, He humbled Himself by becoming obedient to the point of death, even death on a cross." How poor did he become? Second Corinthians 5:21 tells us: "He made Him who knew no sin to be sin on our behalf, so that we might become the righteousness of God in Him."

These fifteen Greek words may be the most profound in the New Testament, and the greatest summary of the doctrine of justification. "He made Him who knew no sin to be sin." What does that mean? Some of the "word of faith" teachers espouse this meaning: on the cross, Jesus became a sinner, and He needed to go to hell for three days to have His sins expiated through punishment, after which God released Him to the resurrection. Is that what it means that He *became* sin?

No—in fact, that's blasphemous. Hanging on the cross, Jesus was as sinless and perfect as ever before or since. If He had been guilty of anything, He couldn't have died for us. He was the spotless Lamb of God, without blemish; He was not a sinner. In what sense, then, was He "made . . . sin"? One simple sense: on the cross, Jesus was guilty of nothing, but the guilt of His people was *imputed* to Him—charged to His account. God treated Jesus as if He personally had committed every sin of every person who would believe. God treated Him that way, though in fact He had committed none of those sins. God exploded the full fury of His wrath against Jesus for all the sins of all who will ever believe, and He exhausted His wrath on Him. He did it on our behalf, in order that we might become the righteousness of God in Him.

That's why Jesus had to live all those years in perfect obedience: He needed to fulfill all righteousness, so that His life could be imputed to us. We're not righteous; we all know that. On the cross, Jesus wasn't a sinner, but God treated Him as if He was. And although you're not righteous, He treats you as if you are—because on the cross, God treated Jesus as if He had lived your life, so that He could treat you as if you had lived His.

That's imputation. That's substitution—perhaps the greatest expression of God's grace to us. Jesus came and became poor to exchange His life for yours, in order to fulfill the elective plan of God, that He might do the will of God perfectly and in the end give back to God the very love gift that the Father had given to Him.

Chapter Two

THE GOD OF THE BIBLE IS SOVEREIGN

O ur God is in the heavens; He does whatever He pleases" (Ps. 115:3). That's a simple but effective look into the nature of God's sovereignty. Over and over, Scripture extols God's sovereign control over every aspect of His creation. "Whatever the Lord pleases, He does, in heaven and in earth, in the seas and in all deeps" (Ps. 135:6). The Apostle Paul explains that God "works all things after the counsel of His will" (Eph. 1:11). And in 1 Corinthians, Paul likewise exalts God as uniquely sovereign: "There is but one God, the Father, from whom are all things, and we exist for Him; and one Lord, Jesus Christ, by whom are all things, and we exist through Him" (1 Cor. 8:6).

The point is unmistakably clear: God reigns as the sovereign Creator and sustainer of the universe, and "from Him and through Him and to Him are all things" (Rom. 11:36).

But any time you deal with the doctrine of God's sovereignty, it sparks an inevitable question. It's a very important question, one that deals with a specific aspect of God's sovereignty and how it relates to His grace in election. In fact, it's probably the most pervasive question in the minds of those who are in the process of embracing the doctrines of grace.

The question is: Does the doctrine of God's sovereignty eliminate any meaningful role for the human will? Does this doctrine suggest that we are mere robots?

Some see an insurmountable contradiction between divine sovereignty and human responsibility. They claim the human will is not truly free in any meaningful sense if it can be overruled by an irresistible divine decree. Arminians and hyper-Calvinists alike have claimed that is the logical conclusion we should draw from the doctrine of divine sovereignty. But that line of reasoning results in a skewed caricature of God's grace through election—one that paints the Lord as a distant, discriminatory tyrant and humans as little more than automatons who function without any will of their own.

The truth, however, is that God exercises His full sovereignty without using force or coercion in any way that would nullify the human will. The 1689 London Baptist Confession of Faith says it this way: "God hath decreed in himself, from all eternity, by the most wise and holy counsel of his own will, freely and unchangeably, all things, whatsoever comes to pass; yet so as thereby is God neither the author of sin nor hath fellowship with any therein; *nor is violence offered to the will of the creature,* nor yet is the liberty or contingency of second causes taken away, but rather established; in which appears his wisdom in disposing all things, and power and faithfulness in accomplishing his decree" (3.1; emphasis added).

We have complete freedom to make choices according to our own nature and preferences. But there's the rub. We don't have sufficient willpower to change our nature (Jer. 13:23). Our own "nature and preferences" guarantee that we will make sinful choices. We're never "forced" by our sovereign God to make the wrong choices that we make. So God's sovereignty does not nullify our own personal responsibility for the sinful things we do.

Still, the relationship between God's sovereignty and human responsibility is not instantly obvious, and at first glance it seems paradoxical. But Scripture offers us considerable insight into how these twin truths harmonize within the plan of redemption.

Divine Sovereignty and Human Responsibility

The first step in understanding the compatibility between God's sovereignty and human will is to recognize that they are *not* mutually exclusive, and Scripture makes this absolutely clear. In God's design, human responsibility is clearly not eliminated by God's sovereign control over His creation. That's true even though evil was included in His grand design for the universe even before the beginning of time, and He uses His creatures' sin for purposes that are always (and only) *good*. Indeed, in His infinite wisdom, He is able to use all things for good (Rom. 8:28).

Consider the Lord's opening statement in Isaiah 10:5: "Woe to Assyria, the rod of My anger." At first glance, this makes no sense. If Assyria is functioning as an instrument of God's judgment, why is He pronouncing condemnation on the Assyrians? "Woe" is an onomatopoeic word (meaning the word sounds like what it means; in this case, a cry of agony) that warns of calamity or massive judgment to come. But how can a people come under divine denunciation and judgment while at the same time functioning as a rod of God's anger? The rest of the verse says, "the staff in whose hand is My indignation." Assyria, this pagan, godless, idolatrous nation, is the instrument of divine judgment against God's own rebellious people.

In fact, the next verse says, "I send it against a godless nation [Judah, the southern part of the kingdom] and commission it against the people of My fury" (v. 6). The Jews are thus designated as the people of God's fury. God holds Israel fully responsible for their disbelief; fully responsible for their idolatry; fully responsible for their rebellion and their rejection of Him, His Word, and His worship. So He commissions the Assyrians to come against them. Notice verse 6: "To capture booty, and to seize plunder, and to trample them down like mud in the streets." That's strong, decisive language.

Now here you have a divine decree in action. God grabs Assyria by the nape of its national neck and assigns it to be the instrument of His fury against the godless people of Judah who have rejected and rebelled against Him. And then He says in verse 7, "Yet it [Assyria] does not so intend, nor does it plan so in its heart." Assyria is the instrument of God's judgment—and the Assyrians themselves are clueless about it. It was never Assyria's purpose, motive, or intention to *serve God*. They had no interest in the God of Scripture—they didn't even believe in Him. Rather, Assyria planned in its own heart to cut off many nations. This was just another opportunity for the Assyrian power to knock off another neighboring nation, as they'd already done to Calno, Carchemish, Hamath, Arpad, Samaria, and Damascus (v. 9). Verses 10 and 11 depict Assyria's confidence in its ability to conquer Judah: "As my hand has reached to the kingdom of the idols, whose graven images were greater than those of Jerusalem and Samaria, shall I not do to Jerusalem and her images just as I have done to Samaria and her idols?" All Assyria knows is that it has destroyed other nations who, in its judgment, had greater protection and greater gods than the God of the Bible. The Assyrians simply intended to do to Judah what they had done to the rest of the nations. They thought they were acting in complete independence. They had no idea that God was using them as agents to deliver His judgment.

But does being instruments of divine wrath somehow exonerate them from responsibility for the evil inherent in their military policies? If this irresistible divine decree brings them to Israel, what culpability do they have for their actions? And yet Scripture is clear that they *will* be held accountable. Verse 12 says that when God has finished using Assyria as an instrument of His fury, "So it will be that when the Lord has completed all His work on Mount Zion and on Jerusalem, He will say, 'I will punish the fruit of the arrogant heart of the king of Assyria and the pomp of his haughtiness.'" The Lord has already decreed that once He is done using Assyria, He will punish it for its sins. The very act that the Assyrians carried out under divine decree was an act of evil—so evil that God will turn on them and bring destruction on them. In God's eyes, they bear full culpability for every part of their evil slaughter and destruction, even though they are fulfilling His divine decree.

Not only did God pronounce judgment on Assyria for its wicked *deeds* but also for the *motives* behind the deeds. "I will punish the fruit of the arrogant heart of the king of Assyria and the pomp of his haughtiness. For he has said, 'By the power of my hand and by my wisdom I did this'" (vv. 12–13). God will punish the Assyrians for their motives and for their failure to recognize His glory by taking credit for what they had done. They thought they had done it by the power of their hands and the wisdom of their own design. Isaiah records the king of Assyria's arrogant boasts:

> By the power of my hand and by my wisdom I did this,
> For I have understanding;
> And I removed the boundaries of the peoples
> And plundered their treasures,
> And like a mighty man I brought down their inhabitants,
> And my hand reached to the riches of the peoples like a nest,
> And as one gathers abandoned eggs, I gathered all the earth;
> And there was not one that flapped its wing or opened its beak or chirped. (vv. 13–14)

That rebellious pride is what invites divine wrath. The Assyrians' motives and arrogance put them in the path of God's judgment. Isaiah vividly depicts the ignorance and foolishness of their haughty attitude.

> Is the axe to boast itself over the one who chops with it?
> Is the saw to exalt itself over the one who wields it?
> That would be like a club wielding those who lift it,
> Or like a rod lifting him who is not wood. (v. 15)

God is the One who wielded Assyria like an ax to chop down Judah and Jerusalem, and yet He righteously holds the ax responsible (vv. 15–18).

Here's the point: although God controls by divine decree and sovereign power everything that goes on in the world according to His own purposes, that does not remove one iota of culpability from those who do evil. Evildoers do evil not because they are forced to, but by their own evil intent. So God will judge them for both the act and the motive, as well as for their failure to give Him glory and to worship Him.

And Isaiah never makes an attempt to resolve or explain away what many would regard as a judicial paradox. Scripture gives no indication that God's wrath against Assyria was anything but just, reasonable, and appropriate. The Bible is simply not concerned with reconciling divine judgment with any human assumptions about justice or fairness. Scripture simply explains what God did, and we are to understand that it was just and fair *because He did it.*

We see the same tension between divine sovereignty and human responsibility in bold relief in Acts 2. During Peter's sermon on the day of Pentecost, he said, "Men of Israel, listen to these words: Jesus the Nazarene, a man attested to you by God with miracles and wonders and signs which God performed through Him in your midst, just as you yourselves know—this Man, delivered over by the predetermined plan and foreknowledge of God, you nailed to a cross by the hands of godless men and put Him to death" (vv. 22–23).

Christ died under God's authority, in His timing, and according to His plan. And yet *Israel* was guilty—both for their collective hand in His death and for their failure to believe in Him as Messiah.

But the guilt of Christ's murder was not isolated to Israel alone. In Acts 4:27, there's another indictment: "For truly in this city there were gathered together against Your holy servant Jesus, whom You anointed, both Herod and Pontius Pilate, along with the Gentiles and the peoples of Israel." The point is clear: Christ's death was a corporate act of sinful humanity aligned together against God. All are guilty.

But the prayer of verse 27 continues in verse 28, saying that all these guilty souls conspired together "to do whatever Your hand and Your purpose predestined to occur." Isaiah 53:10 agrees, identifying the Lord as the One responsible for the Son's death: "The Lord was pleased to crush Him, putting Him to grief." That by no means exonerates the ones who carried out Christ's execution. The perpetrators' intentions were entirely rebellious and murderous, and for them, it was an act of pure evil.

Bearing that in mind, Christ's death is, therefore, the greatest fulfillment of the truth embodied in Joseph's insightful words to his brothers in Genesis 50:20: "As for you, you meant it for evil against me, but God meant it for good." The fulfillment of God's redemptive plan in the death of Christ in no way mitigates the guilt of His murderers. While the Lord ordained and orchestrated every event to bring about His desired ends, the wicked human hands that accomplished the work are no less guilty for the sinful role they played.

We see those seemingly contrasting truths of divine sovereignty and human responsibility repeatedly, in every part of God's Word. But Scripture never attempts to ease the apparent tension. There's no inspired explanation that spells out their complex relationship. Therefore, we need to be careful in attempting to conform God's divine decrees to our own feeble sense of fairness. We need to remember that it's not our job to hold God to whatever standards our meager minds might suggest. He Himself is the standard of true righteousness, and He never acts in a way that would contradict His righteousness or justice.

On Being Born and Born Again

We find a similar tension in John 3. A man named Nicodemus came to see Jesus. He was an important religious ruler of the Jews, and a formidable teacher among the Pharisees. Scripture says he came by night, and we assume that was because he wanted to keep his meeting with Jesus a secret from his fellow religious leaders. He said to Jesus, "Rabbi, we know that You have come from God as a teacher; for no one can do these signs that You do unless God is with him" (v. 2). He grasped the real purpose behind the miracles of Jesus—that they were evidence of His divinity. But Jesus ignored what Nicodemus said and went straight to the question that was truly on his heart (cf. John 2:24). Jesus always knew what people were thinking and He knew what was troubling Nicodemus. The question burdening his heart was, "How do I get into the kingdom of God?" And before Nicodemus could put his question into words, Jesus answered: "Truly, truly, I say to you, unless one is born again he cannot see the kingdom of God" (John 3:3).

That prompted a different question from Nicodemus: "How can a man be born when he is old?" (v. 4). As a Pharisee, Nicodemus knew what it was to speak in analogies and parables—the religious leaders did it all the time. That was the normal pattern of spiritual discourse in those days. He knew it was a spiritual conversation, but he also understood that being born again is not something you can do for yourself. "How can a man be born when he is old?" In other words, the analogy of birth precludes any action on the part of the one that is born. You didn't bring yourself into the world the first time, and you're not going to be able to do it the second time. He understood Christ's analogy, but it hadn't brought him any closer to the answer he sought. Nicodemus wanted to see the kingdom of God, but he needed to be born again. He had to start again at the very beginning with new life, and he knew it was impossible on his own.

Jesus answered him, "Truly, truly, I say to you, unless one is born of water and the Spirit he cannot enter the kingdom of God" (v. 5). Jesus took Nicodemus back to Ezekiel's prophecy of the new covenant, in which God says, "I will sprinkle clean water on you, and you will be clean; I will cleanse you from all your filthiness and from all your idols. Moreover, I will give you a new heart and put a new spirit within you; and I will remove the heart of stone from your flesh and give you a heart of flesh. I will put My Spirit within you and cause you to walk in My statutes, and you will be careful to observe My ordinances" (Ezek. 36:25–27). Christ's words alluded to the nature of new covenant regeneration. He essentially told Nicodemus, "You must be washed, you must be given a new heart, and you must have the Spirit planted in you."

And unless God is the one who sovereignly gives you a new heart, gives you His Spirit, and washes you from above, you can't enter the kingdom. "That which is born of the flesh is flesh, and that which is born of the Spirit is spirit" (John 3:6). Flesh can only produce flesh. The new birth depends on a spiritual work of God. You cannot enter the kingdom unless you are born again, and people can't summon their own spiritual birth.

Moreover, Christ explained that being born again cannot be manufactured or manipulated; it is an entirely divine prerogative. He told Nicodemus, "The wind blows where it wishes" (v. 8). Not only is the new birth available only through God, it's ultimately up to Him when and where He creates new spiritual life.

Understandably dumbfounded and possibly somewhat

disheartened, Nicodemus said to Him, "How can these things be?" (v. 9).

Jesus replied, "Are you the teacher of Israel, and do not understand these things?" (v. 10). Perhaps there is some comfort in knowing that Israel's religious leaders had just as much difficulty understanding God's sovereignty as we do today. Christ's point was not to insult Nicodemus, but to highlight the spiritual bankruptcy of Jewish religiosity, which had devolved into a system of external righteousness and empty piety. Our Lord was setting up a contrast between the legalism of the Pharisees and the true nature of God's saving and transforming work.

If the conversation had ended there, things might have seemed hopeless for Nicodemus—and for every other sinner seeking redemption and forgiveness. But it didn't end there. Christ continued, foreshadowing His own sacrificial death: "Even so must the Son of Man be lifted up; so that whoever believes will in Him have eternal life. For God so loved the world, that He gave His only begotten Son, that whoever believes in Him shall not perish, but have eternal life. . . . He who believes in Him is not judged; he who does not believe has been judged already, because he has not believed in the name of the only begotten Son of God" (vv. 15–18).

Jesus didn't tell Nicodemus that he needed to pray a special prayer; nor did He prescribe several steps to achieve spiritual wholeness. Instead, He simply charged him to *believe*. Christ's words would have been earth shattering for someone who had lived his entire life in a legalistic system of works-righteousness. The message was clear—there was nothing Nicodemus (or anyone else) could do to earn God's favor or produce his own rebirth. It was all a work of God—one that could not be manipulated or manufactured by man. And yet, Nicodemus was responsible to believe. That's the tension in Christ's exhortation to be born again: salvation is entirely God's work, but it is nevertheless our duty to believe, and God will hold those who refuse Him responsible for their unbelief.

We see the same thing a few chapters later in John 6. In verse 37, Christ says, "All that the Father gives Me will come to Me." But in verse 44, He says, "No one can come to Me unless the Father who sent Me draws him." So which is it? Are we saved because we came to Christ, or because God first drew us to the Son? Is salvation open to "whoever believes" (John 3:16), or is it completely out of our control, like the "wind blow[ing] where it wishes" (3:8)?

The answer lies in Christ's metaphor of the new birth. No act of human will can forgive sins, transform hearts, renew minds, or cleanse souls. Apart from the work of God, we have no hope of salvation. Our only option is to echo the cry of the tax collector in Luke 18:13: "God, be merciful to me, the sinner!" But God doesn't perform His redeeming work in opposition to our will, either. He doesn't intervene and inflict His salvation on unwilling recipients. In His perfect plan, He sovereignly draws us to Christ. On our own, we would never choose to believe in Christ. But in God's sovereignty, those He draws will, without fail, believe.

Despite the apparent tension between God's sovereignty and man's responsibility, Scripture never equivocates on presenting these two great realities side by side, working in harmony. In fact, Paul's letter to the Romans *celebrates* it.

The Essentials of Salvation

In Romans 9–11, we see Paul's heart as an evangelist. He had a passion for the salvation of sinners, and it was particularly strong for the Jews—after all, they were his people. So in Romans 9, he starts by saying, "I am telling the truth in Christ, I am not lying, my conscience testifies with me in the Holy Spirit, that I have great sorrow and unceasing grief in my heart" (vv. 1–2). What was Paul so sorrowful about? He explains, "For I could wish that I myself were accursed, separated from Christ for the sake of my brethren, my kinsmen according to the flesh" (v. 3). Paul's heart is broken for lost Jews to the degree that he would wish himself out of fellowship with Christ for the sake of winning their salvation. That's an evangelistic zeal that most of us don't know anything about. He expresses the same longing, still with deep passion, a chapter later: "Brethren, my heart's desire and my prayer to God for them is for their salvation" (10:1). Everything in Romans 9 is sandwiched between those earnest expressions of deep desire for the salvation of his fellow Israelites.

The spiritual waywardness and unbelief of Israel fired up Paul's heart. The Israelites had been given the adoption as sons, the glory, the covenants, the law, the temple, and all the blessings and promises of being God's people. They descended from the fathers—the very line of Christ. But they had rejected all that and more, forfeiting their spiritual inheritance and inviting God's wrath. And Paul desperately wanted to see them saved. He was literally begging God for the salvation of sinners. And that evangelistic zeal drove him all the way to Rome, where he was finally beheaded.

Paul knew as well as anyone what is essential if sinners are to be saved. First, he explains that it requires *divine sovereignty*. He recognized that salvation is a divine work. In 9:6, Paul indicates that some believed that God's plans had failed. But the Word of God has not failed in the unbelief of Israel, and here's why: "For they are not all Israel who are descended from Israel" (v. 6). God never intended to save all of Israel— He has always been selective. Paul explains that the blessing did not extend equally to all of Abraham's offspring—that it came through Isaac, then Jacob. God never made a secret that this was part of His divine plan: "Jacob I loved, but Esau I hated" (v. 13).

Paul anticipates the possible objection to God's selectivity and heads it off. "What shall we say then? There is no injustice with God, is there? May it never be!" (v. 14). That final phrase, *mē genoito*, is the strongest negative in the Greek language. Paul is saying "No, never, not at all." He goes on, "For He says to Moses, 'I will have mercy on whom I will have mercy, and I will have compassion on whom I will have compassion.' So then it does not depend on the man who wills or the man who runs, but on God who has mercy" (vv. 15–16). The Lord's gracious choice of certain people unto eternal life is just that—*His choice*. It's not based on human merit or exertion. To further illustrate God's discriminatory practices, Paul looks all the way back to Pharaoh: "For the Scripture says to Pharaoh, 'For this very purpose I raised you up, to demonstrate My power in you, and that My name might be proclaimed throughout the whole earth.' So then He has mercy on whom He desires, and He hardens whom He desires" (vv. 17–18).

Again, Paul knows our natural inclination is to object on the basis of so-called fairness. In verse 19, he raises the objection for us: "You will say to me then, 'Why does He still find fault? For who resists His will?'" How can God find fault with us if He's the one who makes the decision? How can He harden Pharaoh's heart, then hold him responsible for the actions of a hard heart?

Paul answers those objections by essentially telling us, in his own vernacular, to shut up: "On the contrary, who are you, O man, who answers back to God? The thing molded will not say to the molder, 'Why did you make me like this,' will it? Or does not the potter have a right over the clay, to make from the same lump one vessel for honorable use and another for common use? What if God, although willing to demonstrate His wrath and make His power known, endured with much patience vessels of wrath prepared for destruction?" (vv. 20–22). As the Potter, God exercises ultimate and unquestioned authority over us, the clay.

Now, bear in mind also that God exercises His sovereignty without doing any violence to the will of the creature. Pharaoh was guilty because he himself was in willful rebellion against God. God did not overrule any desire or inclination of Pharaoh in order to harden the evil ruler's heart. The hardening of Pharaoh's heart was not done against Pharaoh's own will.

Still, this passage in Romans 9 is perhaps the strongest statement of divine sovereignty in the New Testament. We must understand that God has the right to put His wrath and His justice on display for His glory just as much as He has a right to put His mercy and His grace on display. Obviously, we prefer the glory that He receives from His grace, but He gets just as much glory from His wrath. It is simply not up to us to determine how God displays His glory. Paul understands that salvation is a sovereign work and that God is not unjust, and nothing here contradicts the truth of Psalm 119:142, which says, "Your righteousness is an everlasting righteousness." God will do what God will do, and it will always be righteous and just.

But then comes Romans 9:30. "What shall we say then? That Gentiles, who did not pursue righteousness, attained righteousness." They weren't even pursuing it, but they received it through faith in Christ. Here we see another juxtaposition between faith and works. "But Israel, pursuing a law of righteousness, did not arrive at that law" (v. 31). Israel was blinded by their legalism, and they rejected the One in whom one must place faith because He was a stumbling stone and a rock of offense to them (1 Peter 2:8).

In addition to divine sovereignty, Paul also understood that salvation requires *faith*. God hardens whom He hardens; He has mercy on whom He has mercy. And yet, Israel is fully responsible for rejecting Christ. Paul says their problem was that "they have a zeal for God, but not in accordance with knowledge" (Rom. 10:2). Israel had fabricated a Jehovah of their own making, just as they had in the wilderness when they made the golden calf. As a result, they had no appreciation for how righteous God is or how sinful they were. They knew God had commanded them to "be holy to Me, for I the Lord am holy" (Lev. 20:26), but they had no idea of what constitutes true holiness. They falsely believed that a grand display of fastidious public piety was the same as true righteousness, and that God was concerned with their outward behavior more than the state of their hearts. In effect, they inflated the value of their own standards while underestimating God's, presuming that they could attain righteousness through their own moral and religious achievements.

Paul says it was a function of their ignorance—that "not knowing about God's righteousness and seeking to establish their own, they did not subject themselves to the righteousness of God" (v. 3). They didn't understand that good works and sacrifices do not merit God's favor (1 Sam. 15:22; Ps. 5:16–17)—that Christ's life brought an end to the law and fulfilled the necessary righteousness for everyone who believes. They didn't understand that Christ frees the penitent believing sinner from the condemnation of the law. They were still trying to achieve a righteousness of their own by the law (Rom. 10:5). But Paul makes it clear in his letter to the Galatians that there is no hope of righteousness or salvation through the works of the law. "For as many as are of the works of the law are under a curse; for it is written, 'Cursed is everyone who does not abide by all things written in the book of the law, to perform them.'

Now that no one is justified by the law before God is evident; for, 'The righteous man shall live by faith'" (Gal. 3:10–11). If you put your hope in your ability to live up to the perfection God's law demands, you are inviting God's wrath and your own damnation.

It should shock us that this chapter on the necessity of faith (Rom. 10) backs right up against chapter 9, with its emphasis on God's sovereignty. Statements like "I will have mercy on whom I have mercy, and I will have compassion on whom I have compassion" (Rom. 9:15) may not seem to harmonize easily with Paul's focus on faith in chapter 10. Consider what Paul writes in 10:11–13: "For the Scripture says, 'Whoever believes in Him will not be disappointed.' For there is no distinction between Jew and Greek; for the same Lord is Lord of all, abounding in riches for all who call on Him; for 'Whoever will call on the name of the Lord will be saved.'" In Paul's mind, and throughout God's Word, these two truths about the necessity of salvation—one stressing God's sovereignty, the other declaring the sinner's responsibility—consistently go together, and no caveats or explanations are given.

Instead, Paul turns to a third essential element of salvation—our *gospel duty*. He writes, "'Whoever will call on the name of the Lord will be saved.' How then will they call on Him in whom they have not believed? How will they believe in Him whom they have not heard? And how will they hear without a preacher? How will they preach unless they are sent? Just as it is written, 'How beautiful are the feet of those who bring good news of good things!'" (vv. 13–15). If you want to understand the marvelous work of salvation, you have to account for all three principles: divine sovereignty, human responsibility, and gospel duty. "And how will they hear without a preacher? How will they preach unless they are sent? Just as it is written, 'How beautiful are the feet of those who bring good news of good things!'" Paul understands that an essential means by which divine sovereignty and human responsibility come together is through our gospel duty as we proclaim the truth.

This is yet another mysterious element in God's sovereign plan. He could simply invade the hearts and minds of those He chose to save, but He didn't. His plan does not conform to the lopsidedness of human reason. In His divine design, His unmerited grace must be met with a positive response of obedient faith. And once redeemed, His people enjoy the privilege of heralding His grace to others. God could have chosen any means to communicate His gospel to the world, but for reasons we can't fully comprehend, He chose us.

The simple truth is that we must adore God and be content to understand Him to the degree that He has permitted us to. We can ask nothing more. We must not foolishly think we deserve more or even dream of making suggestions to Him about how He ought to explain Himself to our satisfaction. We have enough to worship Him and to love Him with all our heart, soul, mind, and strength, and to be lost in wonder, love, and praise.

That's what Paul is doing in Romans 11. Near the end of the chapter, Paul exults, "Oh, the depth of the riches both of the wisdom and knowledge of God! How unsearchable are His judgments and unfathomable His ways!" (v. 33). In the study of God's sovereignty, that's where we all should end up—accepting that we won't ever fully know or understand the mind of God. Psalm 139:6 reminds us that "such knowledge is too wonderful for me, it is too high, I cannot attain to it." God's ways are way beyond us.

But in the same breath, we must acknowledge our love for these rich truths. We love the truth of divine sovereignty. We embrace the truth of human responsibility. And we cherish our gospel duty.

God's sovereignty is one of several truths Scripture teaches about God are that inconceivable, incomprehensible, unfathomable, and unsearchable. It's futile to wish that God had revealed more (or explained more) about how His sovereignty functions without destroying human free agency. But more information wouldn't necessarily answer all our questions anyway. Some truths (like the obvious but incomprehensible concept of infinity) can only be accepted and admired; they can't be condensed and wrapped in a package that fits inside the human brain.

Paul sums that principle up with a rhetorical question, "For who has known the mind of the Lord?" (Rom. 11:34). That ought to give us pause in our search for answers. We'll never wrap our finite intellects around God. His sovereignty is a truth that should provoke wonder and worship. What's clear is that God is completely sovereign, and He never exercises that sovereignty in ways that conflict with or compete with His righteousness, grace, and justice.

Chapter Three

THE GOD OF THE BIBLE IS GOOD AND POWERFUL

One of the most common excuses given by those who reject the God of the Bible is the issue of evil in the world. Skeptics and theological liberals ask, "How can the God portrayed in the Bible as good, holy, and loving allow massive injustices and evil in the world?" Some ask, "How can an all-powerful God be loving *and* tolerate all of the effects of evil which inflict so much suffering around the world?" In fact, many skeptics and theological liberals believe this dilemma backs Christians into an impossible position.

Their argument boils down to a simplistic syllogism: "The biblical God is a loving, benevolent, holy, all-knowing, all-wise, and omnipotent Sovereign who created everything in the universe. If such a God exists, everything should be perfect and good.

"But it is evident that there is much evil in the world. Therefore," they say, "the biblical God does not exist."

But does the presence of evil truly disprove the God of the Bible? Is that really all it takes to upend biblical Christianity?

The Problem of Evil

In reality, the syllogism shows no understanding of what Scripture teaches about evil. The only thing it actually proves is that the person making the argument hasn't read much of the Bible—or simply doesn't recognize the authority of God's Word.

Nevertheless, many evangelical Christians are stymied by arguments like that. They think of the problem of evil as a "fourth and 40 on the ten-yard line" (to borrow an expression from gridiron football). They believe the only good option available to them is to punt—to kick the argument as far away as possible. They might quote Deuteronomy 29:29, which says, "The secret things belong to the Lord our God."

But is a cowering appeal to mystery really a sound biblical answer to the problem of evil?

It's not a good answer at all. In fact, to give an answer like that is to forfeit a wonderful opportunity for explaining the gospel. The existence of evil is not an issue that should put Christians on their heels. The answer to why God allows evil in the world is in the Bible. We can know it, we can thoroughly embrace it, and we can enjoy it. It's not an inadequate short answer, either. It fully accounts for God's benevolence, His omnipotence, His holiness, and His wisdom. And it exalts His glory. In fact, the answer to the problem of evil begins and ends with God and His glory.

This branch of theology is called "theodicy." The term is derived from two Greek words: *theos*, meaning "God"; and *dikaioō*, a word that can mean either "to justify" or "to make or declare righteous." Theodicy is a defense of God's righteousness in light of the reality that evil exists in the universe He created.

Even within the realm of theodicy, there are plenty of wrong answers to the problem of evil. Theological liberals try to rescue God from what they believe is a bad caricature of Him in the Bible. They basically just deny what the Bible says about God and offer their own version of a more true and benign deity. This new god is assembled like a cardboard doll held together with brads, from scraps of their own personality and preferences, then colored to reflect whatever values and morals are important to them. In short, they make a god in their own image.

Others, like process theologians, insist that evil proves that God Himself is imperfect. They argue that His knowledge and power must be limited in some way. They postulate that He is "in process"—getting better as He gets more information.

In the same way, open theism limits God's knowledge. Open theists surmise that the future must be unknown to God—"open" in the sense that it's full of possibilities but unknowable because it hasn't happened yet. The best their god can do is predict the possible outcomes, wait to see what occurs, and respond accordingly. They have essentially created a god without omniscience, whose excuse for evil is his own ignorance.

The common thread across all those aberrant brands of

theology is their man-centeredness—their determination that God's nature cannot and must not offend human sensibilities. Their God must fit within their own presuppositions and preferences. They want to determine who God is and what He is like rather than believing what He has revealed about Himself. They have in effect set themselves above God.

Another common wrong answer to the problem of evil is called metaphysical theodicy, which says good exists, therefore evil *must* exist, because the fact of anything necessarily posits its opposite. Evil is therefore inevitable just because good is a reality, and every yin must have its yang. This is basically a modern version of Zoroastrianism or Manichaeism—two ancient dualistic heresies that taught that two coeternal independent realities, good and evil, are always present. In other words, they believe good and evil are equally ultimate. But according to Scripture, evil is not an eternal reality. It did not exist at all until God's creatures rebelled against their Creator. Furthermore, in the end, evil will be overthrown and eliminated, so the eternity to come will be evil-free. You can't affirm that aspect of biblical theology if you embrace metaphysical theodicy.

The next category of theodicy, the most popular among evangelicals today, is autonomy. Autonomous theodicy teaches that the cause of evil is the abuse of creaturely free will. This is a very sentimental approach. It begins with the assumption that God would never willingly ordain evil; He would not decree a plan for His creation that unleashes so much misery into His universe. They also imagine, evidently, that human free will trumps everything else on God's scale of values, so they often suggest that God had to allow for the possibility of evil in order to protect His creatures' highly prized autonomy. The idea is sometimes articulated this way: "God wants you to love Him all on your own, not because He made you love Him." A God who would willingly permit evil or sovereignly choose whom to save is a God whom some people just can't live with, so they reinvent Him to reflect their own priorities—which in this case means an emphasis on the nobility and value of their own free will that frankly is found nowhere in the Bible.

Perhaps the most obvious problem with the human autonomy argument is that it solves none of the problems theodicy supposedly addresses. Human autonomy, even if existed in this sense, wouldn't really vindicate God by the standard that this view uses as its starting point. Nor does human autonomy really answer the objections people raise against the doctrine of divine sovereignty. Because if God knew in advance that His creatures would sin, He set the plan in motion anyway. All the evil, divine judgment, and determination of eternal punishment were thereby ordained by His choice, because He set these events in motion with full knowledge of the consequences.

So all those different kinds of theodicy are fatally flawed, shortsighted answers. If God has limited power or doesn't have complete knowledge, the universe is out of control at the most crucial point. And if God is not truly omniscient, how can anyone know for certain whether He will ever accumulate the knowledge He needs to curb the effects of evil and conquer it once and for all? Why would anyone prefer a God who is trying to get control of evil rather than a God who is completely in control of it? It's heresy to say the world is full of evil apart from a predetermined plan and purpose of God.

The same goes for most of the answers to the problem of evil—they fail because they attempt to reconcile the truth about God and the existence of evil to the satisfaction of the unbelieving world. They're too focused on rounding off the sharp edges of biblical truth in order to accommodate philosophies and worldviews that are openly hostile to God and His Word—to conform God's goodness and power to the boundaries and limitations of the unilluminated mind (cf. 1 Cor. 1:18; 2:14).

Explanation, Not Accommodation

I want to pursue a different pattern of logic—one centered on explaining the existence of evil, not accommodating it. That means we must deal with what we know to be true.

We start where the Bible starts—with God. He has revealed Himself to be almighty, all-knowing, infinitely good, and in every way glorious. To know Him is to believe in Him as He has revealed Himself. Those who doubt or despise His character don't know Him at all and at best are merely flailing in spiritual darkness in an attempt to explain something they can never know. "Without faith it is impossible to please Him, for he who comes to God must believe that He is and that He is a rewarder of those who seek Him" (Heb. 11:6).

With that in mind, what do we know about evil?

First of all, we know evil exists. Most people, including those who say they believe in the inherent goodness of man, affirm the presence of evil. Evil is an incontrovertible fact. And there are different kinds of evil. First, there is *natural evil*. It is impersonal, external, physical, and temporal. It includes diseases, disaster, catastrophes, weeds, bad weather, tiny bacteria, and everything in between. The whole natural world is cursed and blighted, and we live at the mercy of a fallen creation. No aspect of life is untouched by physical corruption—even the process of aging is evidence that natural evil exists.

A second category of evil is *moral evil*. Moral evil is personal, inside of us, and spiritual. It is wickedness, sin—transgression of God's law (1 John 3:4). Scripture is clear that moral evil dominates human life. "There is none righteous, not even one" (Rom. 3:10). "The intent of man's heart is evil from his youth" (Gen. 8:21). "Each one is tempted when he is carried away and enticed by his own lust. Then when lust has conceived, it gives birth to sin; and when sin is accomplished, it brings forth death" (James 1:14–15). Just as all of creation bears the scars of natural evil, society is overrun with internal evil and corruption. It affects every person and every relationship in every dimension. Human relationships can be very hard to maintain, because they are essentially just collisions of immoral people. Moral evil alone would be enough to engulf us, but there is even more evil.

There is also *supernatural evil*. This is demonic evil. It was our Lord who said to the Jewish leaders, "You are of your father the devil" (John 8:44). The Apostle John says, "The whole world lies in the power of the evil one" (1 John 5:19). This is a supernatural expression of evil against which we wrestle. The Apostle Paul says, "For our struggle is not against flesh and blood, but against the rulers, against the powers, against the world forces of this darkness, against the spiritual forces of wickedness in the heavenly places" (Eph. 6:12). These vile fallen angels are as old as creation. They propagate unmitigated wickedness, and they have plied their supernatural evil on every generation since the creation. They have a temporary, delegated authority in this world system, but their authority is still formidable. They use their powers to seduce and deceive. And they create a kind of cosmos that exploits the corruption that is already in us so that it is fiercely exacerbated.

Second, we know that the God of the Bible exists. There is no other God but the God of the Bible. He is the true and only living God. Because He created the universe, He knows how it operates. He understands reality perfectly. Scripture is His own self-disclosure. It reveals Him to be all powerful. He is all-knowing. He is good. He is loving. He is holy. He is sovereign and controls absolutely everything. There is nothing that exists or occurs or ever will that is not in His control. Over and over, Scripture testifies to this:

> Yours, O Lord, is the greatness and the power and the glory and the victory and the majesty, indeed everything that is in the heavens and the earth; Yours is the dominion, O Lord, and You exalt Yourself as head over all. Both riches and honor come from You, and You rule over all, and in Your hand is power and might; and it lies in Your hand to make great and to strengthen everyone. (1 Chron. 29:11–12)

Our God is in the heavens; He does whatever He pleases. (Ps. 115:3)

All the inhabitants of the earth are accounted as nothing, but He does according to His will in the host of heaven and among the inhabitants of earth; and no one can ward off His hand or say to Him, "What have You done?" (Dan. 4:35)

Thus, Scripture clearly affirms the sovereignty of God. He has the right to govern the universe that He has made, and He does so. He has the right of the potter over the clay. He may mold that clay into whatever form He chooses, fashioning out of the same lump whatever it is that He desires to fashion. He is under no law outside of Himself.

See now that I, I am He, and there is no god besides Me; it is I who put to death and give life. I have wounded and it is I who heal, and there is no one who can deliver from My hand. (Deut. 32:39)

Then the LORD said to him, "Who has made man's mouth? Or who makes him mute, or deaf, or seeing, or blind? Is it not I, the LORD?" (Ex. 4:11)

Who is there who speaks and it comes to pass, unless the Lord has commanded it? Is it not from the mouth of the Most High that both good and ill go forth? (Lam. 3:37–38)

For He spoke, and it was done; He commanded, and it stood fast. The LORD nullifies the counsel of the nations; He frustrates the plans of the peoples. The counsel of the LORD stands forever, the plans of His heart from generation to generation. (Ps. 33:9–11)

The LORD has established His throne in the heavens, and His sovereignty rules over all. (Ps. 103:19)

For the LORD of hosts has planned, and who can frustrate it? And as for His stretched-out hand, who can turn it back? (Isa. 14:27)

The LORD kills and makes alive: He brings down to Sheol and raises up. The LORD makes poor and rich. He brings low, He also exalts. He raises the poor from the dust, He lifts the needy from the ash heap to make them sit with nobles, and inherit a seat of honor; for the pillars of the earth are the Lord's, and He set the world on them. (1 Sam. 2:6–8)

God speaks for Himself in unmistakable terms. He is sovereign over everything that exists, including evil. In Revelation 4:11, those in the throne room of heaven worship God: "Worthy are You, our Lord and our God, to receive glory and honor and power; for You created all things, and because of Your will they existed, and were created."

That is the God of the Bible. The God who is in absolute

control of everything, and nothing—not even sin and evil—can disrupt or derail His plan. The rebellion of Satan and his followers didn't surprise God, nor did the fall of Adam and Eve force Him to resort to plan B. He makes it clear in Isaiah 46:9–10 that His plans will always come to pass: "For I am God, and there is no other; I am God, and there is no one like Me, declaring the end from the beginning, and from ancient times things which have not been done, saying, 'My purpose will be established, and I will accomplish all My good pleasure.'" This is the God who exists.

Third, we know that God is completely perfect, untouched by sin altogether. In Psalm 5:4, David writes, "For You are not a God who takes pleasure in wickedness; no evil dwells with You." God is not susceptible to the temptations of sin (James 1:13). He is light and in Him there is no darkness at all (1 John 1:5).

Taken together, those three facts—that evil exists, that God is sovereign, and that He is utterly holy and righteous—lead us to an inevitable conclusion: that God, in His sovereign wisdom, allows evil to exist without Himself being evil. As the final authority over all creation, God permits evil to exist—not merely with an unwilling acceptance. Evil was part of His plan and eternal decree. He has a purpose in it, and it's a good purpose.

The notion that God has a purpose in evil strikes panic in the hearts of people who have not thought carefully about God's sovereign omnipotence. They can't envision how God might derive glory or fulfill His good purposes by letting evil exist in His universe. They imagine (wrongly) that if God sovereignly ordained a universe that could be cursed with evil, He must be the efficient cause of the evil. They wrongly assume that if God saves some sinners but not all, He must bear the moral responsibility for the fact that some are not saved. They want to rescue God from blame for all the bad things that happen. And having not thought carefully about God's sovereignty and what it means, they wrongly assume that the only way to vindicate God is to reinvent Him. They don't want to imply, of course, that He is not good, loving, holy, or omniscient. Therefore, their own faulty logic forces them to conclude that there must be some limitation to His sovereignty. Some (as we have seen) go so far as to conclude that He doesn't have the power to stop evil. Others believe that He has the power, but some self-imposed limitation keeps Him from using it. They are operating with the assumption that the only way to save God from bad press is by believing that the human will reigns supreme.

But Scripture clearly teaches that while God is not the author or efficient cause of evil, He does exercise control over it. He doesn't in any sense approve of evil, ratify it, look on it with favor, give it His blessing, or delight in it. But nothing happens outside of His sovereignty. Consider the case of Job—God turned Satan loose for horrendous evil in the life of Job. All the suffering Job endured at the hands of Satan happened under the Lord's authority; none of it occurred outside the plan and power of God. None of it could have occurred if God had not willingly permitted it.

We see the same thing in the New Testament, when Jesus said to Peter, "Simon, Simon, behold, Satan has demanded permission to sift you like wheat; but I have prayed for you, that your faith may not fail; and you, when once you have turned again, strengthen your brothers" (Luke 22:31–32). If I had been Peter, I would have said, "Well, You told him no, right?" But Jesus granted Satan permission, knowing that Peter would be strengthened, not destroyed, by the ordeal—and that after enduring the trial, Peter would use his immense leadership skills to strengthen the other disciples.

The Apostle Paul likewise endured Satan's assaults. In 2 Corinthians 12:7, Paul says, "There was given me a thorn in the flesh, a messenger of Satan to torment me—to keep me from exalting myself!" It is evident from the text that the "messenger" in question is a demon. Paul was not possessed by a demon—instead, the demon was leading the false teachers who were pillaging the Corinthian church. Paul prayed three times that it might be removed, and the Lord did not remove it. Paul says twice that God didn't answer his prayer because it was His purpose "to keep me from exalting myself" (v. 7). If God so designs, He will use a demon-led false teacher to inflict trouble on a complacent church or to humble a pastor. In His sovereign control, He can use anything to bring about His desired ends. When we look at it from the perspective of the biblical facts, we see that the problem of evil is no problem at all for God, because He is totally sovereign over evil and neither His power nor His glory is in any way threatened by it.

For His Glory and Our Good

The real question then is *why?* Why did God permit evil in the first place? Why does He sovereignly, willingly allow it to keep infecting and distorting His creation? In His unfolding, preordained plan, what is the presence of evil accomplishing?

In his epistle to the Romans, Paul gives us the answer. He writes, "If our unrighteousness demonstrates the righteousness of God, what shall we say?" (Rom. 3:5). Our unrighteousness demonstrates (Greek *sunistēmi*) the righteousness of God. In the context of Romans, Paul has been showing that God is faithful to His promises to Israel despite their sin and unbelief. Compared to the rebellious wickedness of Israel, God's righteousness is truly and unmistakably glorious. And that's the bottom line: We would never understand the full glory of God's righteousness if we were not so familiar with the wretched fruits of unrighteousness.

Unrighteousness therefore puts God's righteousness on display. Paul again says, "But God demonstrates His own love toward us, in that while we were yet sinners, Christ died for us" (Rom. 5:8). The presence of sin allows God to demonstrate His righteousness and love. How else could He show the character of His great love that rescues enemies and sinners if there were no sinners and enemies? "What if God, although willing [i.e., determining] to demonstrate [Greek *endeiknumi*] His wrath and to make His power known, endured with much patience vessels of wrath prepared for destruction?" (Rom. 9:22). He demonstrates His righteousness against the backdrop of sin and evil, showing, by contrast, how utterly holy He is. God demonstrates His love at a level that would have been impossible without sin. We see and appreciate the radiance of God's love more, having endured the darkness and distress of a universe cursed by evil. "The people who walk in darkness will see a great light; those who live in a dark land, the light will shine on them" (Isa. 9:2). The presence of evil provided the perfect opportunity for God to display His wrath and justice along with His redeeming grace and infinite mercy, as He loved sinners enough to send His Son to die in their place.

But God's demonstration of His righteousness and wrath against the backdrop of evil is not merely for our benefit. The word "demonstrate" in Romans 9:22 is an aorist middle in the Greek. Literally, the verse's phrasing is "God determined to demonstrate *for Himself*." God demonstrates His attributes for the sake of His own glory. Without sin, God's wrath would never be on display. Without sinners to redeem, God's grace would never be on display. Without evil to punish, God's justice would never be on display. And He has every right to put Himself everlastingly on display in all the glory of all His attributes.

On the other hand, God finds no pleasure in the death of the wicked (Ezek. 33:11). Trust me: God hates evil more than you do. But Paul says He endures sin with patience. "Endures" is a passive verb. God keeps Himself distant from the acts of evil agents while remaining fully sovereign over them. God endures this horrible assault on His everlasting holiness. He endures the horrifying blasphemy throughout the history of fallen humanity. Why? For the sake of His glory.

Jude says, "For certain persons have crept in unnoticed, those who were long beforehand marked out for this condemnation" (v. 4). The everlasting condemnation of these apostates was written before history began. God foreordained the existence of evil (though, again, He is never the efficient cause of it). He did it for the purpose of putting on display the majesty of His holiness. Unrighteousness has colored our whole earthly existence, and through our deliberate sins, we have been willing participants in it. If it weren't for the fact of our fallen existence, we wouldn't know very much about God's everlasting righteousness—much less be able to give Him glory for it. We wouldn't know that He is as loving as He is if it weren't for our sin. We wouldn't know that He is as holy as He is if it weren't for the reality of divine judgment. And a host of other divine attributes would be largely obscured by the sheer brilliance of God's glory if we weren't able to see Him in stark contrast against the backdrop of evil.

In Romans 9:23, Paul further explains God's patience with sin: "And He did so to make known the riches of His glory upon vessels of mercy, which He prepared beforehand for glory." In Jude 4, the apostates' condemnation was prepared beforehand, whereas Paul says that the vessels of mercy were also prepared beforehand. That is why the Lamb was slain before the foundation of the world (Rev. 13:8). He did all of this in order that He might gather into heaven a redeemed humanity who would forever glorify Him for all that He is.

The murder of Christ is unquestionably the greatest evil ever committed. But under the preordained plan of God, that act of supreme wickedness was also a supreme display of His grace, mercy, wrath, justice, righteousness, and countless other attributes. It gives us a glimpse into His loving character that we otherwise never would have seen. And revealing those aspects of His nature in turn causes us to love and glorify Him more.

In short, God tolerates sin and evil because, in the end, it brings Him more glory.

Chapter Four

THE GOD OF THE BIBLE IS HOLY

We can't fully understand God's holiness. But we can understand it much better than we currently do. By and large, the typical evangelical's understanding of God is pathetically superficial. Too many professing believers think about God in only self-centered and self-indulgent terms, reducing Him to little more than a genie in a lamp. Others are preoccupied with a relational perspective on God. They want Him to be more comfortable and inviting—less of a divine sovereign and more of a casual buddy. Such shallow thinking invites confusion and corruption into the midst of God's people and perverts their perspective of their holy Lord and Savior.

In fact, today most of the dominant errors in the church spring from a lack of respect and appreciation for God's holiness. We can do a lot to inoculate ourselves from bad theology and heresy simply by cultivating a biblical perspective on God's utterly holy nature.

To begin, we need to see His holiness as more than just another attribute. A.A. Hodge said, "The holiness of God is not to be conceived of as one attribute among others; it is rather a general term representing the conception of His consummate perfection and total glory. It is His infinite moral perfection crowning His infinite intelligence and power."[1] Thomas Watson said, "Holiness is the most sparkling Jewel of his Crown; it's the Name by which God is known, Psal. 111.9."[2] R.L. Dabney wrote, "Holiness, therefore, is to be regarded, not as a distinct attribute, but as the resultant of all God's moral attributes together. . . . His holiness is the collective and consummate glory of His nature as an infinite, morally pure, active, and intelligent Spirit."[3] In Isaiah 57:15, the prophet reports, "For thus says the high and exalted One Who lives forever, 'whose name is Holy.'"

God's being is utterly separate from ours, and Scripture makes that clear. He is *being* and we are *becoming*. The Hebrew word for holiness is *qadosh*; the Greek is *hagios*. Both have the connotation of something that is distinct and separate. Therefore, nothing in the creation compares to God in His essential nature. He is wholly other than His creatures. He is incomparable. He is infinite perfection. That is why Exodus 15:11 says, "Who is like You, majestic in holiness?" First Samuel 2:2 says, "There is no one holy like the Lord, indeed, there is no one besides You." The psalmist says, "Holy and awesome is His name" (Ps. 111:9).

The Expression of God's Holiness

It's hard for us to comprehend the difference between *being* and *becoming*. God's moral perfection and sinlessness are fixed and immutable. In that regard, His holiness is nothing like the holiness of the saints. We who believe are being conformed to the image of Christ, but our sanctification is always in process. We're being stripped of our former sinfulness and refined through the work of the Spirit into conformity to God's righteousness. By contrast, God is, will be, and always has been utterly holy and perfect, totally separate from any stain of unrighteousness. As the prophet Habakkuk wrote, "Your eyes are too pure to approve evil. And You cannot look on wickedness" (Hab. 1:13). Job 34:10 says, "Far be it from God to do wickedness, and from the Almighty to do wrong." God's holiness is therefore unique—singularly and eternally perfect. In Revelation 15:4, the Apostle says, "You alone are holy."

Scripture doesn't just talk about God's holiness; it *reveals* His holiness. In fact, every revelation of God is a revelation of His moral perfection. We could study God's holiness by studying creation. At the end of creation, Moses reports, "God saw all that He had made, and behold, it was very good" (Gen. 1:31). This is a reflection of His essential nature. Scripture records on each day that creation was good, but in the end when God saw creation in its totality, it was not just good, but *very* good. In fact, Ecclesiastes 7:29, speaking directly of man, says, "God made men upright." Of course, He could do no other. Whatever came from His being had to be perfect. Made in His image, man was free from sin.

We could study the law of God and its revelation of His absolute perfection. In Psalm 19:7, David says, "The Law of the Lord is perfect." In Romans 7:12, the Apostle Paul says, "The Law is holy, and the commandment is holy and righteous and good."

We could also study God's holiness in His judgment. All His verdicts and adjudications from the divine bench are holy. "Shall not the Judge of all the earth deal justly?" (Gen. 18:25). In 2 Timothy 4:8, Paul refers to Him as "the Lord, the righteous Judge."

Or we could study God's holiness by catching a glimpse of heaven. In Revelation 4, we are taken into the heaven of heavens. John, in the Spirit, sees a throne standing in heaven, "and One sitting on the throne. And He who was sitting was like a jasper stone and a sardius in appearance; and there was a rainbow around the throne, like an emerald" (vv. 2–3). He continues:

> Around the throne were twenty-four thrones; and upon the thrones I saw twenty-four elders sitting, clothed in white garments, and golden crowns on their heads. Out from the throne come flashes of lightning and sounds and peals of thunder. And there were seven lamps of fire burning before the throne, which are the seven Spirits of God; and before the throne there was something like a sea of glass, like crystal; and in the center and around

the throne, four living creatures full of eyes in front and behind. The first creature was like a lion, and the second creature like a calf, and the third creature had a face like that of a man, and the fourth creature was like a flying eagle. And the four living creatures, each one of them having six wings, are full of eyes around and within; and day and night they do not cease to say, "Holy, holy, holy is the Lord God, the Almighty, Who was and Who is and Who is to come." (vv. 4–8)

In heaven, when God's holiness is mentioned in worship, the word is multiplied three times: "Holy, holy, holy" (cf. Isa. 6:3). No doubt, the threefold expression of praise is a Trinitarian reference, but it also emphasizes the utter and absolute distinction of God's moral perfection. God can only manifest that which is absolutely holy, and thus James says, "Every good thing given and every perfect gift is from above, coming down from the Father of lights, with whom there is no variation or shifting shadow" (James 1:17). There is no wavering or fluctuation in the absolute holiness of God. There are no flaws or irregularities in its perfect brilliance. It is, as He is, constant and consummately dazzling.

Holiness and Humanity

The most discernable manifestation of God's holiness is starkly contrasted against the blackest backdrop. God reveals His holiness in the incarnation. John tells us that when Jesus came, He was declared to be God. In John 1:18, the Apostle says, "No one has seen God at any time; the only begotten God who is in the bosom of the Father, He has explained Him." Whatever you want to know about God is explained in the person of Jesus. Hebrews 1 says:

> God, after He spoke long ago to the fathers in the prophets in many portions and in many ways, in these last days has spoken to us in His Son, whom He appointed heir of all things, through whom also He made the world. And He is the radiance of His glory and the exact representation of His nature, and upholds all things by the word of His power. (vv. 1–3)

In Luke 1, Gabriel comes to Mary and makes the great announcement about the birth of the Son of God, the Christ. As befitting His holiness, His incarnation would be unique.

> The angel said to her, "Do not be afraid, Mary; for you have found favor with God. And behold, you will conceive in your womb and bear a son, and you shall name Him Jesus. He will be great and will be called the Son of the Most High; and the Lord God will give Him the throne of His father David; and He will reign over the house of Jacob forever, and His kingdom will have no end." Mary said to the angel, "How can this be, since I am a virgin?" The angel answered and said to her, "The Holy Spirit will come upon you, and the

power of the Most High will overshadow you; and for that reason the holy Child shall be called the Son of God." (vv. 30–35)

The Holy Spirit and the Holy Father sent the Holy Offspring, the Son of God. He was supernaturally conceived in order to preserve His holiness and keep Him distinct from the fallen line of Adam. He was truly and fully human, but without the fallen nature we inherit from Adam. The angel told Mary, "The Holy Spirit will come upon you, and the power of the Most High will overshadow you; and for that reason the holy Child shall be called the Son of God" (Luke 1:35). The angel likewise told Joseph: "The Child who has been conceived in her is of the Holy Spirit" (Matt. 1:20). Contrast that with David's statement in Psalm 51:5 that "in sin my mother conceived me."

But it wasn't only in Christ's birth that He was set apart. Consider Luke's account of the Lord's baptism. Luke makes it clear that the Father and Spirit were present, testifying to Christ's holiness. "Now when all the people were baptized, Jesus was also baptized, and while He was praying, heaven was opened, and the Holy Spirit descended upon Him in bodily form like a dove, and a voice came out of heaven, 'You are My beloved Son, in You I am well-pleased'" (Luke 3:21–22). The Father intervenes on the proceedings to affirm the Son's divinity and moral perfection. Contrast that with Peter's charge in Acts 2:38: "Repent, and each of you be baptized in the name of Jesus Christ for the forgiveness of your sins."

Christ's holiness is further revealed in His death. In 2 Corinthians 5:21, Paul says, "He made Him who knew no sin to be sin on our behalf, so that we might become the righteousness of God in Him." The Apostle Peter says, "knowing that you were not redeemed with perishable things like silver or gold from your futile way of life inherited from your forefathers, but with precious blood, as of a lamb unblemished and spotless, the blood of Christ" (1 Peter 1:18–19). Whether you're looking at His birth, His baptism, or even His death, His holiness is manifest.

Defending the use of the sign of the fish (the *ichthus*) as a reference to the Lord, Augustine explained it is a suitable sign for Christ because "He was able to live, that is, to exist, without sin in the abyss of this mortality as in the depths of waters."[4] Christ literally came down and sunk Himself in this wretched world. The truest test of holiness is not how it holds up in heaven but how it holds up here.

And His holiness did hold up, in spite of the wretchedness of the world around Him. In John 8:46, Jesus said, "Which one of you convicts Me of sin?" In John 14:30, Jesus said of Satan, "The ruler of this world is coming, and he has nothing in Me." He wasn't merely saying that Satan had nothing *on* Him, but that there was nothing at all *in* Him that responded to Satan. There was never the slightest possibility that He would compromise His holiness.

Theologians commonly use two similar Latin phrases to make an important distinction in their discussions of Christ's impeccability. He is *non posse peccare* (not able to sin), not merely *posse non peccare* (able not to sin). His holiness as a perfect man was not merely the happy result of His supernaturally empowered human self-control. His absolute sinless perfection was the necessary corollary of the fact that He possessed both divine and human natures. As God incarnate, Christ could no more sin than God can tell a lie, and "God . . . cannot lie" (Titus 1:2). "He cannot deny Himself" (2 Tim. 2:13). "Jesus Christ is the same yesterday and today and forever" (Heb. 13:8). His perfect, immutable, divine holiness made it impossible for Him to sin—not because he lacked any of the human faculties or natural weaknesses that make us susceptible to temptation, but because His revulsion for sin is so utterly absolute and His divine holiness is so gloriously superlative.

Scripture is loaded with warnings about living in this world, because unlike Christ, we are easily susceptible to the enticements of sin, even though we are redeemed. We may have been walking in the faith for many years and consistently studying the Bible for a long time, but this world is still a threat to us at every turn. Old habits, human weaknesses, and carnal desires remain with us—and will be there until we are fully glorified. That's why we so easily respond to Satan and the world. Consequently, we must be regularly reminded *not* to love the world. We must be reminded *not* to walk in the counsel of the wicked, stand in the path of sinners, or sit in the seat of scoffers (Ps. 1:1). Not heeding Scripture's repeated warnings would have devastating results for us.

That's why the example of Christ's holiness is such an

encouragement. While we'll never live up to His holy perfection, we ought to look at the world and its temptations the way He saw them. In Mark 7:18, Jesus says, "Are you so lacking in understanding also? Do you not understand that whatever goes into the man from outside cannot defile him?" It doesn't matter what came at Jesus. Nothing external could defile Him because only what's in the heart defiles. He goes on to say, "For from within, out of the heart of men, proceed the evil thoughts, fornications, thefts, murders, adulteries, deeds of coveting and wickedness, as well as deceit, sensuality, envy, slander, pride and foolishness. All these evil things proceed from within and defile the man" (vv. 21–23).

We need to take sin seriously. Paul tells the Corinthian church that they must remove the sinning man out of their church because "a little leaven leavens the whole lump" (1 Cor. 5:6). If they allowed sin to reside unchecked in their church, it would corrupt the whole body. That's why church discipline is important. We live a fragile existence in this wretched world. We must watch our lives. We must press our body into submission. We must guard our eyes. We must keep our feet from going certain places. We must keep our distance from certain people. We must live a circumspect life in this world so that we do not put ourselves in a position to be assaulted by temptation and devastated by the ravages of sin. When people ask me what appeals to me about heaven, it isn't streets of transparent gold or gates made of pearls; it's the absence of sin. I'm tired of sin.

Bad Company Could Not Corrupt Christ

Not only did Christ's holiness stand up to the test of the world's corruption, it also withstood the presence of vile sinners and reprobates. Luke's gospel records that some of Christ's closest associates—even some of the disciples—were notorious sinners. "After that He went out and noticed a tax gatherer named Levi" (Luke 5:27). This is Matthew, and he was a small-time tax gatherer. He was a *mokhes*, not a *gabbai*—a knuckle-crusher, not a Mafia boss. A *gabbai* was a big-time tax collector who owned a regional tax franchise from Rome and hired these little *mokhes* guys to do the dirty work. Often, they sat at a crossroads and taxed the wheels on your cart, the beasts of burden that pulled the cart, the letters you were carrying, the goods you bought, and anything else they could think of. They extorted everything they could from everyone, not only to give the prescribed rate to Rome but also to make their own fortune. They were in collusion with the Roman government and oppressors of their own people. As a result, they had all been banned from the temple in Jerusalem and excommunicated from the synagogues in every town. In effect, they had traded their birthright for a mess of pottage (cf. Gen. 25:29–34).

Jesus comes to Levi, perhaps the last person on the planet you would ever choose to be a disciple of the Messiah, and says, "Follow Me" (Luke 5:27). So Levi jumped up from his tax table and followed Him. Verse 29 tells us Levi had a big party at his house, and a great crowd of his fellow tax collectors and other sinners gathered. They were all reclining at the table, enjoying the feast. And the Pharisees, with all their legalistic scruples, grumbled at Jesus' disciples, "'Why do you eat and drink with the tax collectors and sinners?' And Jesus answered and said to them, 'It is not those who are well who need a physician, but those who are sick'" (vv. 30–31).

In Matthew 11:19, Jesus reports on what people were saying about Him: "Behold, a gluttonous man and a drunkard, a friend of tax collectors and sinners!" But while He was a friend to sinners, He never adopted their vices or imitated their lifestyles. He remained utterly holy in every encounter. Jesus went into the most contagious sick ward on the planet and emerged unscathed. He was the living cure for every disease. He told the Pharisees, "I have not come to call the righteous but sinners to repentance" (Luke 5:32). This is the greatest illustration of the holiness of Jesus. He could hang around the most wretched people in the society, and it never had a corrupting influence on Him. He had the opposite effect on others.

Luke further illustrates the consistency of Christ's holiness in the seventh chapter of his gospel, during another dinner meeting, this time at the home of a Pharisee. Christ didn't mind being with the self-righteous hypocrite—just as He had elsewhere with more overt sinners, Jesus entered his home and reclined at the table. The houses tended to be open, and a meal would be going on with the dignitaries and people in the community allowed to stand around the outside and listen to the conversation. Luke tells us, "There was a woman in the city who was a sinner; and when she learned that He was reclining at the table in the Pharisee's house, she brought an alabaster vial of perfume" (Luke 7:37). For a prostitute, this was a part of her operation. In Proverbs, Solomon describes prostitutes as perfuming their beds (Prov. 7:17). And she must have been a fairly successful prostitute, because her perfume was in a valuable alabaster vial. Luke paints the scene as she approached Christ:

> Standing behind Him at His feet, weeping, she began to wet His feet with her tears, and kept wiping them with the hair of her head, and kissing His feet and anointing them with the perfume. Now when the Pharisee who had invited Him saw this, he said to himself, "If this man were a prophet He would know who and what sort of person this woman is who is touching Him, that she is a sinner." (Luke 7:38–39)

The Pharisee jumped to conclusions out of the experience of his own heart. What sinful man is going to have a prostitute do that to his feet without having an illicit thought? But instead of the woman corrupting or tempting Jesus, Scripture says, "Then He said to her, 'Your sins have been forgiven.' Those who were reclining at the table with Him began to say to themselves, 'Who is this man who even forgives sins?' And He said to the woman, 'Your faith has saved you; go in peace'" (vv. 48–50).

Publicly, she was known for the worst kind of immorality and filthiness, but she was on a mission of repentant worship. She had no water, so she used her own tears. (Luther famously called her tears *Herzwasser*, or "heart water.") The only thing approximating cloth she had was her hair, so that's what she used. The only gift she could give was what she used for her immoral relationships. It had no effect on Christ at all except to draw forgiveness out of Him. Unlike the Pharisees and other religious elites, Christ was not susceptible to the weaknesses of the flesh. Scripture says:

> For it was fitting for us to have such a high priest, holy, innocent, undefiled, separated from sinners and exalted above the heavens; who does not need daily, like those high priests, to offer up sacrifices, first for His own sins and then for the sins of the people, because this He did once for all when He offered up Himself. For the Law appoints men as high priests who are weak, but the word of the oath, which came after the Law, appoints a Son, made perfect forever. (Heb. 7:26–28)

Face-to-Face with the Holy One

Not many human eyes have ever glimpsed the full manifestation of God's holiness and glory. Even fewer have lived to tell the tale. In Isaiah 6, the Old Testament prophet brings us along with him into the throne room of heaven. Verse 1 sets the context, saying it happened "in the year of King Uzziah's death."

Uzziah became king at age sixteen and reigned for fifty-two years under God's continual blessing. It was a time of unusual peace and prosperity in Judah—the best of times (other than the era of Jehoshaphat's reign) since the time of Solomon. But Uzziah sinned by intruding into the priest's office, and he was smitten by God with leprosy. The disease ultimately proved fatal, and when Uzziah died, the outlook was grim.

Isaiah went to the temple to seek God, and he was given a vision of heaven. He writes, "I saw the Lord sitting on a throne, lofty and exalted, with the train of His robe filling the temple. Seraphim stood above Him, each having six wings: with two he covered his face, and with two he covered his feet, and with two he flew" (vv. 1–3). In an antiphonal pattern, "one called out to another and said, 'Holy, holy, holy is the Lord of hosts, The whole earth is full of His glory'" (v. 3).

> And the foundations of the thresholds trembled at the voice of him who called out, while the temple was filling with smoke. Then I said,
> "Woe is me, for I am ruined!
> Because I am a man of unclean lips,
> And I live among a people of unclean lips;
> For my eyes have seen the King, the Lord of hosts."
> Then one of the seraphim flew to me with a burning coal in his hand, which he had taken from the altar with tongs. He touched my mouth with it and said, "Behold, this has touched your lips; and your iniquity is taken away and your sin is forgiven." (vv. 4–7)

"Woe is me" is not a phrase Isaiah used lightly, nor was it a plea for sympathy. A chapter earlier, he had used the word "woe" six times to describe God's curse of damnation against the unfaithfulness of Judah. Now Isaiah himself stood face-to-face with the Lord, and he saw himself as cursed—because he saw his own sin and was overwhelmed. In a literal translation of the Hebrew, Isaiah said, "I am disintegrating because I have a dirty mouth." He was affirming his depravity and the depravity of his people in light of God's incomprehensible holiness. He was filled with despair because he had seen the King of kings and Lord of hosts.

But when the seraphim placed a burning coal on his lips, it depicted the application of the atonement. He was purified.

> Then I heard the voice of the Lord, saying, "Whom shall I send, and who will go for Us?" Then I said, "Here am I. Send me!" He said, "Go, and tell this people:
>> 'Keep on listening, but do not perceive;
>> Keep on looking, but do not understand.
>> Render the hearts of this people insensitive,
>> Their ears dull,
>> And their eyes dim,
>> Otherwise they might see with their eyes,
>> Hear with their ears,
>> Understand with their hearts,
>> And return and be healed.'" (vv. 8–10)

God told Isaiah he would meet resistance. Naturally, Isaiah asked, "Lord, how long?" (v. 11). God answered:

Until cities are devastated and without inhabitant,
Houses are without people
And the land is utterly desolate. . . .
Yet there will be a tenth portion in it. . . .
Whose stump remains when it is felled.
The holy seed is its stump. (vv. 11, 13)

The Apostle John says,

These things Jesus spoke, and He went away and hid Himself from them. But though He had performed so many signs before them, yet they were not believing in Him. This was to fulfill the word of Isaiah the prophet which he spoke: "Lord, who has believed our report? And to whom has the arm of the Lord been revealed?" For this reason, they could not believe, for Isaiah said again, "He has blinded their eyes and He hardened their heart, so that they would not see with their eyes and perceive with their heart, and be converted and I heal them." These things Isaiah said because he saw His glory, and he spoke of Him. (John 12:36–41)

That is an amazing statement. John says Isaiah saw the glory of Jesus (v. 37). The One seated on the throne in Isaiah is Christ—He is the One whom the angels perpetually hailed as "holy, holy, holy." The same blazing, shining, majestic God before whom Isaiah trembled took on frail, human flesh, concealed His glory, and humbled Himself in the form of a man. The exalted Lord of heaven is our High Priest who sympathizes with our infirmities, who triumphed over evil, and whose perfection has become our salvation. It is Him we love and serve. We must be overwhelmed by the glory of our Christ and His utter holiness. To Him we give all the glory.

Chapter Five

THE GOD OF THE BIBLE IS LOVING

One time on the Larry King program, I was sitting between Father Michael Manning and Deepak Chopra. We were talking, and Father Manning said, "*My* Jesus loves everybody." Larry King looked at me and said, "You don't feel that way about Jesus, do you, John? You think if people don't believe in Jesus and Jesus alone they're going to hell, right?"

Some people question if Christians can affirm the love of God and still believe in hell. On the surface, the idea that God is love is the most tolerable and universally affirmed truth about Him. Almost everyone is happy that God is love as long as the definition of love is broad and simplistic. But that's because the modern concept of love is so off base, so self-involved and self-indulgent, and so bound up in fleeting emotions and feelings.

God's love isn't any of those things. But our understanding

of love has been so distorted and perverted by worldly influences that even most professing Christians do not understand the depth and the riches of God's love. And we'll never truly know God if we don't attempt to push past the faulty sentimentalism of this world and embrace the profound complexity of His love.

The Nature of God's Love

Scripture clearly testifies that God is love (1 John 4:8). It's not an isolated characteristic—in fact, we see God's love displayed across the full panoply of His attributes. We can start to get our arms around the biblical concept of divine love by breaking it down into three categories.

First, God loves Himself. This is an intra-Trinitarian love, and it is the starting point for every feature of God's love. Before there was any creature to love, God was still the perfect embodiment of love, and divine love was perfectly expressed within the Trinity. In John 14, Scripture says one of the reasons for Christ's incarnation was to put this intra-Trinitarian love on display in terms that humanity could perceive and appreciate: "But so that the world may know that I love the Father, I do exactly as the Father commanded Me" (v. 31). Jesus progressed toward the inevitability of the cross so that the world would know that He loved the Father. He showed us His love for the Father by His perfect, sacrificial obedience.

In John 15, Jesus says, "Just as the Father has loved me, I have also loved you; abide in My love. If you keep My commandments, you will abide in My love; just as I have kept My Father's commandments and abide in His love. These things I have spoken to you so that My joy may be in you, and that your joy may be made full" (vv. 9–11). Again, Jesus demonstrates perfect love in perfect obedience. He says, "I in them and You in Me, that they may be perfected in unity, so that the world may know that You sent Me, and loved them, even as You have loved Me . . . and I have made Your name known to them, and will make it known, so that the love with which You loved Me may be in them, and I in them" (vv. 23, 26).

From Jesus to the Father, His love is connected to the obedience of our Lord. But how does the Father demonstrate His love to the Son?

Therefore Jesus answered and was saying to them, "Truly, truly, I say to you, the Son can do nothing of Himself, unless it is something He sees the Father doing; for whatever the Father does, these things the Son also does in like manner. . . . For just as the Father raises the dead and gives them life, even so the Son also gives life to whom He wishes. For not even the Father judges anyone, but He has given all judgment to the Son, so that all will honor the Son even as they honor the Father. He who does not honor the Son does not honor the Father who sent Him. Truly, truly, I say to you, he who hears My word, and believes Him who sent Me, has eternal life, and does not come into judgment, but has passed out of death into life. Truly, truly, I say to you, an hour is coming and now is, when the dead will hear the voice of the Son of God, and those who hear will live. For just as the Father has life in Himself, even so He gave to the Son also to have life in Himself; and He gave Him authority to execute judgment, because He is the Son of Man." (John 5:19, 21–27)

Everything the Father has He gave to His Son. Everything. The Father shows the Son everything He is doing, and the Son does what He sees the Father doing (5:19). The magnanimity of the love of God to the Son is that all the Father's knowledge, all the Father's power, all the Father's secrets, all the Father's privileges, and all the Father's honor is given to the Son. The Father holds nothing back. And the Son, in perfect reciprocal love, says that all He has is only what the Father has given Him. Thus, He celebrates the expression of perfect love in consummate generosity that holds nothing back.

As we discussed earlier, the Father loves the Son so much that He gives to the Son a redeemed humanity. In the redemptive plan of God, loving His Son is the primary motivation, and loving sinners is secondary. In John 6:37, Jesus says, "All that the Father gives Me will come to Me, and the one who comes to Me I will certainly not cast out." The Father loves sinners so that by loving them, He can express His love to His Son. We're nothing but the Father's love gift as the elect bride to the Son.

While that supernatural, intra-Trinitarian love is primarily expressed in the language between the Father and the Son, it does not leave out the Holy Spirit. Because God the Father perfectly loves the Son, salvation is planned in eternity past. The Father sets aside a bride for His Son. The Son perfectly obeys and loves the Father and is willing to pay the immense price of redemption for His bride. He obeys the Father's will out of love; He becomes a substitute; and He receives the wrath of God for all who would believe. Then, through the work of the Holy Spirit, the Son's bride is saved and sanctified, as believers are fitted for an eternity of worshipful adoration for the Lord. In the end, God's love for sinners rises out of His loving desire to redeem a bride for the Son as an expression of His love.

God's Comprehensive Love

Scripture testifies to a second dimension of God's love—His love for the world. There is an unlimited, indiscriminate kind of love that God extends to all people. In Titus 3:4, the Apostle Paul says God's love—translated in most versions as "kindness" (Greek *chrēstotēs*)—extends to "mankind," meaning the entire human race. When the sinful world interacts at all with God, or God with them, His love will be manifest in some fashion, as His love is a fundamental part of that relationship.

If you want proof that God's love extends to all mankind, look no further than Matthew 5:44–45, where Jesus says, "I say to you, love your enemies and pray for those who persecute you, so that you may be sons of your Father who is in heaven." Never are we more like God than when we love and forgive our enemies. His love is not restricted to the redeemed, and ours should not be either.

We see God's unconditional, indiscriminate love displayed primarily in four ways. The first is what theologians call *common grace*. Extolling God's lovingkindness to all His creatures, Jesus said, "For He causes His sun to rise on the evil and the good, and sends rain on the righteous and the unrighteous. For if you love those who love you, what reward do you have? Do not even the tax collectors do the same?" (Matt. 5:45–46). Christ's point was that it is easy to love those who already love you—even wretched sinners like the tax collectors could do that. But God loves those who don't love Him, and His love is manifest not just in the rain and the sun, but in a variety of earthly, physical, and temporal fashions.

Even life itself is an expression of God's common grace. God told Adam that in the day he ate of the fruit of the tree he would die (Gen. 2:17), but Adam lived for more than nine hundred years (Gen. 5:5). God expresses His love for us through common grace by the very fact that the unregenerate wake up in the morning, smell the coffee, have a good breakfast, kiss the person they love, hug their children, go off to a stimulating career, drive a comfortable car, and enjoy a sunset. Even those who suffer through poverty, hunger, and abuse in this life still enjoy a measure of God's common grace. He loves all men unconditionally in this way. We have to understand that the joys of everyday life are all expressions of God's love. In Acts 14:17, Paul says, "[God] did not leave Himself without witness, in that He did good and gave you rains from heaven and fruitful seasons, satisfying your hearts with food and gladness." That's common grace—that all men, regardless of the nature of their hearts, can live an enjoyable, comfortable life.

The second way God loves humanity is through *compassion*. You can think of God's compassion as part of the motivation behind His common grace, but it extends beyond mere physical and temporal blessings. God also shows His compassion through universal pity and grief over lost souls. In Ezekiel 18:32, God says, "I have no pleasure in the death of anyone who dies." Jeremiah reports these sorrowful words from the Lord:

Listen and give heed, do not be haughty,
For the Lord has spoken.
Give glory to the Lord your God,
Before He brings darkness
And before your feet stumble
On the dusky mountains,
And while you are hoping for light
He makes it into deep darkness,
And turns it into gloom.
But if you will not listen to it,
My soul will sob in secret for such pride;
And my eyes will bitterly weep
And flow down with tears,
Because the flock of the Lord has been taken captive.
(Jer. 13:15–17)

God is weeping through the eyes of Jeremiah. Later on, He weeps and wails over the destruction of Moab (Jer. 48:30–47).

Moab was justly cursed, but God found no pleasure in its iniquity or judgment. At the end of the book of Jonah, God rhetorically asks hard-hearted Jonah, "Should I not have compassion on Nineveh?" (Jonah 4:11).

Throughout His public ministry, Christ reflected God's compassionate love for people. In Matthew 23:37, Jesus cries out, "Jerusalem, Jerusalem, who kills the prophets and stones those who are sent to her! How often I wanted to gather your children together, the way a hen gathers her chicks under her wings, and you were unwilling." In Luke 19:41, Scripture says, "He saw the city and wept over it." He also wept over the tomb of Lazarus (John 11:35). The Lord wept not because Lazarus died—that was by God's design for the sake of the miracle Christ would soon work. In fact, Jesus stayed by the Jordan until the appointed time for Him to leave. Instead, Jesus was weeping because He was face-to-face with the horrible consequence of sin, namely death for all. God's compassionate love is motivated not by the present value of someone but by their lost value that has been forfeited to sin.

The third way God pours out His unconditional love on humanity is through *warning*. All throughout Scripture, God incessantly warns mankind of the judgment that awaits if they do not repent and believe. Luke 13:1–5 recounts one such warning from Christ Himself:

Now on the same occasion there were some present who reported to Him about the Galileans whose blood Pilate had mixed with their sacrifices. And Jesus said to them, "Do you suppose that these Galileans were greater sinners than all other Galileans because they suffered this fate? I tell you, no, but unless you repent, you will all likewise perish. Or do you suppose that those eighteen on whom the tower in Siloam fell and killed them were worse culprits than all the men who live in Jerusalem? I tell you, no, but unless you repent, you will all likewise perish."

In 1 Timothy 4:10, Paul says God "is the Savior of all men, especially of believers." Of course, God won't save everyone eternally, but He is the Savior of all mankind in a physical and temporal sense. He withholds from sinners what they deserve: immediate punishment. The gospel's general call offers Christ as Savior indiscriminately to all who hear—and there is no other Savior. In that sense, Christ is set forth by the Father as the only "Savior of the world" (1 John 4:14).

Why does God withhold His righteous wrath and declare His willingness to save any and all who come? Some suggest that the offer cannot be well meant and that God's only design is to increase the guilt of the reprobate when they refuse the invitation and spurn the command to repent. They think it compromises the sovereignty of God to suggest that He has any goodwill whatsoever toward those whom He permits to continue in sin and unbelief. But the overall effect of common grace will not be to magnify the sinner's guilt or intensify his damnation, because one of the key features of common grace is its restraining effect on the expression of human depravity.

Common grace keeps sinners from being as bad as they might otherwise be (cf. 2 Thess. 2:6–7).

And Scripture is clear about this: God is not insincere. His kindness toward the reprobate is true benevolence, not a veil for pure wrath and undiluted hatred. "The LORD is good to all, And His mercies are over all His works" (Ps. 145:9). In Romans 2:4, Paul says "the kindness of God" ought to lead sinners to repentance. That's the sincere and unfeigned message of common grace. God is holding back judgment and damnation for the sake of those who will still repent and believe. Meanwhile, the sheer kindness shown in His patience ought to draw sinful men and women to Him. Both the Old and New Testaments are filled with vivid, urgent, well-meant warnings about the wrath to come. And each of those warnings is an expression of God's benevolent love for His creatures.

Thus, the fourth way that God shows His love for humanity is through the *free offer of the gospel*. Christ's final charge to His disciples was an order to spread the good news of the gospel throughout the whole world: "Go therefore and make disciples of all the nations" (Matt. 28:19). God's love is evident in that the way of salvation has been made known to people far and wide, across the millennia.

But God makes Himself known not only through evangelism and gospel ministry. Paul explains, "That which is known about God is evident within them; for God made it evident to them" (Rom. 1:19). He has sovereignly implanted evidence of His existence into the very nature of man, both in his ability to reason and in the moral law written on his heart (Rom. 2:15).

We don't have the luxury (or, perhaps, the burden) of knowing ahead of time whom God has elected for salvation. So according to Scripture, we must operate on the basis that every sinner we meet, if he or she believes in Jesus, will be pardoned and saved. "For this is the will of My Father, that everyone who beholds the Son and believes in Him will have eternal life, and I Myself will raise him up on the last day" (John 6:40). The divine Savior is therefore proclaimed to sinners indiscriminately. It's our job to see to it that the glorious news of His gospel reaches to the ends of the earth. We must proclaim Christ to the nations.

> O taste and see that the Lord is good; how blessed is the man who takes refuge in Him! (Ps. 34:8)

> I permitted Myself to be sought by those who did not ask for Me; I permitted Myself to be found by those who did not seek Me. I said, "Here am I, here am I," to a nation which did not call on My name. I have spread out My hands all day long to a rebellious people. (Isa. 65:1–2)

> Jesus spoke to them again in parables, saying, "The kingdom of heaven may be compared to a king who gave a wedding feast for his son. And he sent out his slaves to call those who had been invited to the wedding feast,

and they were unwilling to come. Again he sent out other slaves saying, 'Tell those who have been invited, "Behold, I have prepared my dinner; my oxen and my fattened livestock are all butchered and everything is ready; come to the wedding feast."' But they paid no attention and went their way. . . . [So the king said to his servants,] 'Go therefore to the main highways, and as many as you find there, invite to the wedding feast.' Those slaves went out into the streets and gathered together all they found, both evil and good; and the wedding hall was filled with dinner guests." (Matt. 22:1–5, 9–10; cf. Luke 14:16–24)

In God's loving mercy, He uses us to extend the offer of the gospel into the darkest corners of the world. Our job is to shine the light of His truth. He decides how and where it illuminates men's hearts. In John 5:39–40, Jesus said to the religious leaders, "You search the Scriptures because you think that in them you have eternal life; it is these that testify about Me; and you are unwilling to come to Me so that you may have life." God loved the world so much that He provided a sufficient Savior (John 3:16), but sinners refused to come and are held guilty for that refusal (v. 19).

God has graciously, lovingly extended the offer of the gospel to all mankind. But that offer won't last forever. As Christ Himself said, "Therefore I said to you that you will die in your sins; for unless you believe that I am He, you will die in your sins" (John 8:24).

Love in God's Family

That brings us to the third category of God's love. God not only loves Himself within the Trinity and loves all of humanity, but He also loves His own.

God genuinely loves the world. He loves them enough to give them common grace, to feel compassion for them, to warn them of the coming judgment, and to offer the gospel freely to all. That love has no limit in extent, but it does have a limit in degree. He loves and saves, in a temporal sense, all men, but He uniquely loves and saves believers for eternity. This love is based on nothing but sovereign determination—He's chosen us as Christ's eternal bride, saved and transformed us into new creations, and, as our Father, He loves us as His own children.

Christ's interaction with His disciples on the night of His arrest gives us a precious example of the love God has for His own. In John 13, Jesus is on the brink of His own death, and gathered in the upper room with His obstinate disciples. They're there to celebrate the Passover, and only Christ knows how little time He has left with His friends—they're utterly oblivious to the significance of the moment. John writes, "Now before the Feast of the Passover, Jesus knowing that His hour had come that He would depart out of this world to the Father, having loved His own who were in the world, He loved them to the end" (v. 1). The love of Christ for His disciples—and indeed, for all His people still in the world—extends beyond common grace and mercy. It's a perfect, eternal, saving love.

The Spirit chose a marvelous place in the account of Scripture to have John express this truth, because the disciples in the upper room were having a childish argument about which of them was going to be the greatest in the kingdom. They're so self-centered, immature, selfish, and ambitious that it blinds them to everything else that's going on. Jesus had been warning them about what was going to happen. In the upper room, He sits in the shadow of the cross, with the dark specter of God's wrath falling over Him, and all they can think about is their own glory.

Here, in one of their ugliest moments, when they are utterly indifferent to His imminent crucifixion, Scripture says Jesus loved them "to the end" (Greek *eis telos*). That expression means He loved them to the absolute maximum. Another way to say it would be He loved them to the extreme fullness of His capacity to love them. He could not have loved them more.

And Christ's love for His disciples is astonishing. In the aftermath of the upper room and His arrest, the disciples deserted and denied Him. They were ashamed of Him, and in fear for their own lives, they scattered like disloyal cowards. Real love is demonstrated by obedience. That very night, Jesus had told the disciples, "If you love Me, you will keep My commandments. . . . If anyone loves Me, he will keep My word" (John 14:15, 23). That's how Jesus loved His Father. The disciples failed to show obedient love for their Lord, but Jesus still loved them in spite of their disloyalty.

In the intimacy of the upper room, Jesus pledged His love to them. Moreover, He showed His love to them by washing their filthy feet, even as they debated who was the greatest. A short while later, He would prove just how much He loved them by dying in their place and suffering the due penalty of their sins. "Greater love has no one than this, that one lay down his life for his friends" (John 15:13). God's love for His children is eternal and unfathomably deep. It's a love that longs to protect and preserve His people and ultimately enjoy eternal fellowship with them. As Jesus said to His disciples on the night of His arrest:

> Do not let your heart be troubled; believe in God, believe also in Me. In My Father's house are many dwelling places; if it were not so, I would have told you; for I go to prepare a place for you. If I go and prepare a place for you, I will come again and receive you to Myself, that where I am, there you may be also. And you know the way where I am going. (John 14:1–4)

Jesus didn't oversell heaven, nor did He undersell it. Instead, He faced the sin-bearing agony of the cross like a father who loses himself in the love of his children even as he faces down his own death. He could approach the horrors of Calvary and endure separation from the Father because He knew for whom He was going to the cross—He knew what His sacrifice was purchasing. In His immense love for His own, He willingly marched to His dreadful death. This is what the hymn writer described when he wrote, "The love of Jesus, what it is, none but His loved ones know."[1] This is God's love for His people.

And to our everlasting relief, Paul writes in Romans 8:38–39 that nothing can ever separate us from God's covenant love.

Ezekiel 16 provides us with a wonderful illustration of God's love for His own:

> Then the word of the Lord came to me, saying, "Son of man, make known to Jerusalem her abominations and say, 'Thus says the Lord God to Jerusalem, "Your origin and your birth are from the land of the Canaanite, your father was an Amorite and your mother a Hittite."'" (Ezek. 16:1–3)

This is a basic address to Jerusalem and Israel for their abominations and idolatries. The Amorite and the Hittite are general names for people who dwelt in Canaan. God is referring to the pagan origins of the people of Israel, pointing out that they were once no better than their idolatrous neighbors. The imagery here is vivid—God describes Israel in its earliest days as an abandoned baby.

> As for your birth, on the day you were born your navel cord was not cut, nor were you washed with water for cleansing; you were not rubbed with salt or even wrapped in cloths. No eye looked with pity on you to do any of these things for you, to have compassion on you. Rather you were thrown out into the open field, for you were abhorred on the day you were born. (vv. 4–5)

When a baby was born, he was washed, cleansed, rubbed with salt as a disinfectant, wrapped carefully in cloth, and cared for tenderly. God says He had compassion on Israel because they were like an infant who had been cast aside and not properly been cared for.

"When I passed by you and saw you squirming in your blood, I said to you while you were in your blood, 'Live!' Yes, I said to you while you were in your blood, 'Live!' I made you numerous like plants of the field. Then you grew up, became tall and reached the age for fine ornaments; your breasts were formed and your hair had grown. Yet you were naked and bare. Then I passed by you and saw you, and behold, you were at the time for love; so I spread My skirt over you and covered your nakedness. I also swore to you and entered into a covenant with you so that you became Mine," declares the Lord God.

"Then I bathed you with water, washed off your blood from you and anointed you with oil. I also clothed you with embroidered cloth and put sandals of porpoise skin on your feet; and I wrapped you with fine linen and covered you with silk. I adorned you with ornaments, put bracelets on your hands and a necklace around your neck. I also put a ring in your nostril, earrings in your ears and a beautiful crown on your head. Thus you were adorned with gold and silver, and your dress was of fine linen, silk and embroidered cloth. You ate fine flour, honey and oil; so you were exceedingly beautiful and advanced to royalty. Then your fame went forth among the nations on account of your beauty, for it was perfect because of My splendor which I bestowed on you," declares the Lord God.

"But you trusted in your beauty and played the harlot because of your fame, and you poured out your harlotries on every passer-by who might be willing. You took some of your clothes, made for yourself high places of various colors and played the harlot on them, which should never come about nor happen. You also took your beautiful jewels made of My gold and of My silver, which I had given you, and made for yourself male images that you might play the harlot with them. Then you took your embroidered cloth and covered them, and offered My oil and My incense before them. Also My bread which I gave you, fine flour, oil and honey with which I fed you, you would offer before them for a soothing aroma; so it happened," declares the Lord God. "Moreover, you took your sons and daughters whom you had borne to Me and sacrificed them to idols to be devoured. Were your harlotries so small a matter? You slaughtered My children and offered them up to idols by causing them to pass through the fire. Besides all your abominations and harlotries you did not remember the days of your youth, when you were naked and bare and squirming in your blood." (vv. 6–22)

God's accusation goes on and on like that, describing Israel's horrible waywardness. At one point, He says Israel was even more corrupt than Samaria (vv. 46–47). With shameless abandon, Israel flaunted herself before all the idols of the surrounding nations and spurned the covenant love and grace of God. The description of Israel's rebellion concludes in verses 58 and 59, as Ezekiel writes, "'You have borne the penalty of your lewdness and abominations,' the Lord declares. For thus says the Lord God, 'I will also do with you as you have done, you who have despised the oath by breaking the covenant.'"

You might assume Israel is about to face the wrath they have invited through their wicked rebellion. But the first word in verse 60 is truly amazing: "Nevertheless, I will remember my covenant with you in the days of your youth, and I will establish an everlasting covenant with you." In spite of all their spiritual infidelity, God is gracious to the people of His covenant. Sodom was destroyed, and Samaria disappeared unredeemed. But Israel was worse than both of them, yet God forgave Israel. For those whom He chooses to love in a covenant way, God's love is perfect, complete, saving, and eternal.

Scripture repeatedly extols the glory of God's covenant love. In Jeremiah 31:3, God says, "I have loved you with an everlasting love; therefore I have drawn you with lovingkindness." Before the foundation of the world, God set His love upon His own, and He loves them with an inexhaustible, everlasting love. In Ephesians 2, Paul says this kind of love forgives, gives life, promises eternal glory, grants to us kindness, and produces righteous behavior—all as a function of God's grace.

In Ephesians 5, he says it's a love that cleanses us, purifies us, makes us holy, nourishes us, and cherishes us for eternity. In Luke 15, the parable of the prodigal son pictures God's saving love as it lavishes blessing, rejoices in our repentance, forgives past sin, restores us, and elevates us to a position of rich privilege. And as we already saw in Romans 8, Paul says that this kind of love is inseparable and unconquerable.

The Limits of God's Love

Reflecting on the riches of God's love for His people often leads to the question, "Why did God not choose to love everyone like that?"

While the heart behind that question may be pure (as opposed to cynical and unbelieving), we need to remember not to hold God to the standards of our feeble minds. Every time we pose a question about the *why* of God's ultimate sovereign determination, we are stepping outside our limits.

But in this case, Scripture provides an answer. The reason God did not choose to love everyone equally with His saving, covenant love is because His love is guided and controlled by His glory (Rom. 9:22–24). God is not obligated to be the unqualified, equal-opportunity Savior of everyone. He is not the prisoner of His love, nor of man's expectations. God's love is never separated as superior or dominant over all His other attributes. In the end, it pleased Him to do as He did because it glorified Him. His sovereign plan of redemption is bound up in nothing more than His glory. And in that knowledge we can rest.

Besides, if we understand the true nature of sin, righteousness, and judgment, we should realize that it's no mystery at all why God condemns sinners. The real mystery is why He saves anyone at all.

If the gospel is for some a Savior of life unto life, it is because God determined that it should be. While He feels compassion for all, warns all, and calls all through the preaching of the gospel, He is still glorified in the salvation of some and the condemnation of others.

The glory of His saving work wouldn't shine as brightly if it weren't viewed against the backdrop of His judgment. In the end, it's *His* glory. We must be satisfied in that, and let God be God. When God pardons us, and we escape death based on that pardon, we don't go around questioning whether such pardons were granted to everyone. We grab our pardon and run free joyfully, safe in the grip of His covenant love forever.

Chapter Six

THE GOD OF THE BIBLE
IS A SAVING GOD

John 3:16 may be the most familiar verse in all of Scripture, but it is surely one of the most abused and least understood. The verse is so well known that some Christians seem to think the reference alone is a sufficient proclamation of the gospel. For years, someone in multicolored clown hair could be seen at practically every major sporting event holding a sign saying, "John 3:16," strategically positioned in view of television cameras. There's no evidence those stunts ever really did anything to advance the gospel. They did seem to popularize John 3:16 as a favorite cheer for people who presume on God's love and do not really love Him in return.[1]

Arminians extract the phrase "God so loved the world" from its context and use it as an argument for universal atonement. More extreme universalists push the same argument even further. They claim the verse proves that God loves everyone exactly the same and that He is infinitely merciful—as if John 3:16 negated all the biblical warnings of condemnation for the wicked.

To think like that is to miss the point completely. The immediate context (v. 18) gives the necessary balance: "He who does not believe has been judged already, because he has not believed in the name of the only begotten Son of God." Surely, that is a truth that needs to be proclaimed to our generation with at least as much passion and urgency as the message of God's love and mercy.

Furthermore, John 3:16 says nothing specific about the extent of the atonement; it is a statement about the magnitude of God's love. Here is a profound wonder: God loved "the world"—this wicked realm of fallen humanity—*so much* that He sacrificed His only begotten Son to pay the price of redemption for all who would ever believe in Him.

The Apostle John was staggered by the magnitude of God's love and its implications. He stressed it so much and wrote about it so frequently that he is often called "the Apostle of love." This comment from 1 John 3:1 makes a fitting commentary on the central point of John 3:16: "See how great a love the Father has bestowed on us, that we would be called children of God." The language is as simple as the truth is profound: "how great"! John doesn't employ a dozen adjectives, because all the superlatives in human language wouldn't even come close to declaring the full truth. He simply calls our attention to the inexpressible wonder of God's saving love. The God we worship loves to save.

The Apostle Paul was captivated by the same truth: "Christ died for the ungodly. For one will hardly die for a righteous man; though perhaps for the good man someone would dare even to die. But God demonstrates His own love toward us, in that while we were yet sinners, Christ died for us" (Rom. 5:6–8).

The Apostle Peter mentions "things into which angels long to look" (1 Peter 1:12). One of the pressing questions the angels surely must ponder is why God would pour out His love on fallen humanity. Certainly, no higher authority than God compelled Him to love us.

And fallen humans alone are the recipients of divine mercy: "It is not angels that he helps, but he helps the offspring of Abraham" (Heb. 2:16). "God did not spare angels when they sinned, but cast them into hell and committed them to pits of darkness, reserved for judgment" (2 Peter 2:4).

Why would God choose to love finite, fallen, sinful human beings at the cost of His own Son's life? Why didn't God just write us all off as wretched sinners, make us the objects of His wrath, and display His glory in judgment against us? It is truly a mystery even angels might find bewildering.

Moreover, why is it that He lavishes us with the very riches of His goodness? Couldn't God have displayed His mercy in a lesser way than giving His Son to die for us? Or having redeemed us and guaranteed us entry to heaven, couldn't He have given us a lesser position? Yet, He has made us joint heirs with Christ. He has elevated us to the spiritual heights. Indeed, He has already given us His very best. He has already bestowed the most priceless, eternal blessing in all the universe—His own beloved Son. Therefore, we can be absolutely confident that He will withhold no good thing from us. "He who did not spare his own Son but delivered him over for us all, how will he not also with him freely give us all things?" (Rom. 8:32).

Have you ever truly pondered the mystery of such great love? Why is it that God's greatest love isn't bestowed on the faithful angels who never fell and who steadfastly throughout all time have been loyal to love and worship the God who made them?

In short, why would God even love us, much less pay so high a price to demonstrate His love?

Frankly, the full answer to that question is still shrouded in mystery. It is an immense, incomprehensible wonder. We do not know the reasons God chooses to love fallen sinners. And I must confess, together with each true child of God, that I do not know why God chose to love me. I know only that it is for His own glory, and certainly not because He finds me deserving of His love. In other words, the reasons for His love are to be found in God alone, not in those whom He loves.

And what Scripture reveals is that the will to save is intrinsic to who God is. "God is love" (1 John 4:8, 16). It is not foreign to His nature to be a Savior—to seek and to save the lost. He is a Savior by nature. First Timothy 1:1 refers to the Father as "God our Savior." One of the most vivid verbal images Jesus ever gave to describe God is the eagerness of the father in the parable of the prodigal son. This father looks intently for his lost son's return, runs to meet the wayward boy when he returns, and lavishes him with undeserved gifts and status. That is the very character of the God we worship. He is a saving God.

And He has always been known as a Savior. Theological liberals try to put a great gulf between the New Testament and the Old Testament. They often claim that the God of the Old Testament is an angry, vengeful, envious, vitriolic, hostile, punishing kind of deity. The God revealed in the New Testament is different—a compassionate, loving, saving deity. That's a foolish and dishonest corruption of Scripture.

The God of the Old Testament was known to His people as a Savior. Israel knew God as a Savior—a saving God. To use another word, He is a Deliverer. He rescues people from bondage and death.

Of course, that's not how it is in the science of ethnology and the world of religion and deities. Study ancient Middle Eastern religions and you're not going to find gods who save. Virtually every man-made religious system ever known features some means by which the worshiper by his own efforts can save himself—or, at the very least, better himself. But you're not going to find any man-made god who is by nature a Savior, a rescuer.

For example, in Old Testament times, *Baal* was what the Canaanites named their deities. The Hebrew expression *ba'al* was taken from a Phoenician word meaning "lord," and when the name was used by itself, it was usually a reference to the sun god. Each Canaanite tribe or locality supposedly had its own distinctive god. *Baal-zebub*, for example, was the god of Ekron (2 Kings 1:2–3, 6, 16). His name meant "lord of the flies," and he was so thoroughly foul and filthy that his name was adapted, turned into a pun, and used in New Testament times as a name for Satan: *Beelzebul,* meaning "lord of dung" (Mark 3:22).

The Canaanite Baals were not interested in saving anyone. They could be plied for favors with sacrifices, but it was deemed contrary to the very idea of a deity to imagine that an offended deity himself would take the initiative to provide salvation, forgiveness, or deliverance to anyone who had incurred the wrath or disfavor of the gods.

Elijah's encounter with the priests of Baal on Mount Carmel shows the stark contrast between YHWH and Baal. Elijah proposed a contest:

> "I alone am left a prophet of the Lord, but Baal's prophets are 450 men. Now let them give us two oxen; and let them choose one ox for themselves and cut it up, and place it on the wood, but put no fire under it; and I will prepare the other ox and lay it on the wood, and I will not put a fire under it. Then you call on the name of your god, and I will call on the name of the Lord, and the God who answers by fire, He is God." And all the people said, "That is a good idea." (1 Kings 18:22–24)

So, in a classic characterization of Baal, the priests of Baal tried everything they could think of to get Baal to react. Of course, there is no Baal, so he couldn't do anything because he doesn't exist. Even the demons who might play to people's superstitions and impersonate Baal were unable to effect the necessary miracle. Elijah therefore mocked them, driving them into a mad frenzy.

> It came about at noon, that Elijah mocked them and said, "Call out with a loud voice, for he is a god; either he is occupied or gone aside, or is on a journey, or perhaps he is asleep and needs to be awakened." So they cried with a loud voice and cut themselves according to their custom with swords and lances until the blood gushed out on them. (vv. 27–28)

The best that could be said about Baal (or any other man-made deity) would be that he's indifferent. That's what Elijah's mockery implied. In effect, "Your god is occupied with other things and isn't even listening to you." The Baal priests' frantic efforts ended in bloody exhaustion, with no answer at all from Baal.

The pagan spectrum swings all the way over from indifference to hostility. The Ammonites in the Old Testament worshiped a god named Molech. He was a viciously angry deity who was so evil that the only way to appease him was by child sacrifices. He was depicted by a massive bronze idol. It was hollow, and it was engineered to serve as a fire pit. It would be heated like a furnace, and newborn infants would be cast into the flames as a sacrifice. The Old Testament portrays the ritual slaughter of infants as the most grotesque of all human evils.

Somewhere on that spectrum from apathy to vicious hostility are all the gods of the world. Not one of them is a Savior like YHWH. Unlike all of them, He is compassionate, merciful, tender-hearted, filled with lovingkindness and eager to save people. That lesson was built into the meaning of the Passover, the exodus, the promised Messiah, and all the priestly and sacrificial liturgies.

The psalms are full of this truth: "The LORD is gracious and merciful; Slow to anger and great in lovingkindness. The LORD is good to all, And His mercies are over all His works" (Ps. 145:8–9). "For You, Lord, are good, and ready to forgive, And abundant in lovingkindness to all who call upon You" (86:5). "For the LORD is good; His lovingkindness is everlasting And His faithfulness to all generations" (100:5). Each of the twenty-six verses in Psalm 136 ends with the phrase, "For His lovingkindness is everlasting."

Notice how often when the subject is God's mercy, the Bible stresses His faithfulness and immutability. Indeed, God—as Savior of His people—is the one true constant in all the universe. This is why He redeems His people rather than summarily destroying them when they sin: "For I, the LORD, do not change; therefore you, O sons of Jacob, are not consumed" (Mal. 3:6).

His wrath against sin is real, but it does not provoke Him to alter His Word, revise His will, revoke His promises, or change His mind: "God is not a man, that He should lie, Nor a son of man, that He should repent; Has He said, and will He not do it? Or has He spoken, and will He not make it good?" (Num. 23:19).

The necessary implication of God's immutability is that

He is not subject to shifting moods, flashes of temper, fluctuating dispositions, or seasons of despondency. In theological terms, God is impassible. That means He cannot be moved by involuntary emotions, suffering, pain, or injury. In the words of the Westminster Confession of Faith, God is "infinite in being and perfection, a most pure spirit, invisible, without body, parts, or passions" (2.1).

Steadfast, Not Stony

Divine impassibility is not an easy concept to grasp. Robert Ingersoll, the famous nineteenth-century skeptic, wrote, "Think of that!—without body, parts, or passions. I defy any man in the world to write a better description of nothing. You cannot conceive of a finer word-painting of a vacuum than 'without body, parts, or passions.'"[2] Nowadays, even some Christian theologians shun the idea of divine impassibility because they think it makes God seem cold and aloof.

But that's a false notion. To say that God is not vulnerable, that He Himself cannot be hurt, and that He isn't given to moodiness is not to say He is utterly unfeeling or devoid of affections. Remember, Scripture says God is love, and His compassion, His lovingkindness, and His tender mercies endure forever. "The LORD's lovingkindnesses indeed never cease, For His compassions never fail. They are new every morning; Great is Your faithfulness" (Lam. 3:22–23).

The main problem in our thinking about these things is that we tend to reduce God's attributes to human terms, and we shouldn't. We're not to imagine that God is like us (Ps. 50:21). His affections, unlike human emotions, are not involuntary reflexes, spasms of temper, paroxysms of good and bad humor, or conflicted states of mind. He is as deliberate and as faithful in His lovingkindness as He is perfect and incorruptible in His holiness.

The unchangeableness of God's affections is—or should be—a steady comfort to true believers. His love for us is infinite and unshakable. "As high as the heavens are above the earth, so great is His lovingkindness toward those who fear Him" (Ps. 103:11). His constant mercy is a secure and dependable anchor—both when we sin and when we suffer unjustly. "Just as a father has compassion on his children, so the LORD has compassion on those who fear Him" (v. 13). Far from portraying God as unsympathetic and untouched by our suffering, Scripture emphasizes His deep and devoted compassion virtually every time it mentions the unchangeableness of God.

Notice that I have quoted almost entirely from Old Testament texts to establish the connection between God's compassion and His immutability. The commonly held notion that the Hebrew Scriptures portray God as a stern judge whose verdicts are always unrelentingly severe is an unwarranted caricature. In fact, God's lovingkindness is often given particular emphasis in the very places where His fiery wrath against sin is mentioned (e.g., Neh. 9:17; Ps. 77:7–10; Isa. 54:8; 60:10; Hab. 3:2). Even the prophets' most severe threats and harshest words of condemnation are tempered with reminders of God's inexhaustible kindness and sympathetic mercy (Jer. 33:5–11; Hos. 14:4–9).

Of course, there's a careful balance that must be maintained here. It is neither wise nor helpful to pit the divine attributes against one another as if they were contradictory (they are not) or to act as if God's merciful attributes automatically overruled the gravity of divine justice (they do not). "Behold then the kindness and severity of God" (Rom. 11:22). All of God's attributes are equally—and infinitely—exalted in Scripture.

It is a serious mistake, for example, to pit God's power against His tenderness or imagine that His righteousness conflicts with His mercy. The converse is true as well, and this is the salient point: God's power cannot be correctly understood apart from His benevolence. In fact, God's power is best seen in His tenderness toward the helpless, because His power is made perfect in weakness (2 Cor. 12:9).

The True Meaning of the Gospel

Of course, God's fullest self-revelation as Savior came in the person of Jesus Christ—God in human flesh. The incarnation itself was an expression of sympathy and identification with our weakness (Heb. 4:15). In Christ, we can see countless expressions of divine compassion translated into human idioms that we easily understand and identify with—including sadness, sympathy, and tears of sorrow. Though sinless Himself, Jesus suffered all the consequences of sin in infinite measure—and in so suffering, He identifies with the misery of all who feel the pains of human anguish. This was the whole reason God the Son became a man: "He had to be made like His brethren in all things, so that He might become a merciful and faithful high priest in things pertaining to God, to make propitiation for the sins of the people. For since He Himself was tempted in that which He has suffered, He is able to come to the aid of those who are tempted" (Heb. 2:17–18). "For we do not have a high priest who cannot sympathize with our weaknesses, but One who has been tempted in all things as we are, yet without sin" (4:15).

Those statements show that divine mercy extends far beyond empathy merely for our physical sufferings. Of course, the lovingkindness of God includes a heartfelt concern for our temporal, earthly, physical welfare—but it is infinitely more than that. Both the compassion of God and the earthly work of Christ must be seen ultimately as redemptive. In other words, our Lord's tenderest mercies are concerned primarily with the salvation of our souls, not merely the suffering of our bodies.

Nevertheless, because illness, disability, pain, and all other forms of physical suffering are effects of the fall and fruits of the curse of sin, God's sympathy for the human plight includes a special grace toward those who suffer physically. We see vivid evidence of that in the healing ministry of Jesus. Physical healing was not the central point of His earthly mission. He came, of course, "to seek and to save that which was lost" (Luke 19:10)—to provide redemption and eternal life for sinners. His one message was the gospel, beginning with a call to repentance (Matt. 4:17) and culminating in the promise of eternal rest for weary souls (11:29). But along the way, He encountered multitudes of sick, lame, blind, and other physically suffering people. He healed "every kind of disease and every kind of sickness among the people" (Matt. 4:23; cf. 15:30–31), including congenital disabilities (John 9; Mark 7:32–35); chronic, medically hopeless cases (Luke 8:43–47); and cases of severe demon possession (Mark 5:1–16).

Those physical healings were vivid displays of both Jesus' power and His compassion. They were proof of His deity and living demonstrations of His divine authority. They established His unlimited ability to liberate anyone and everyone from the bondage, the penalty, and the consequences of sin. As such, the healing ministry of Jesus was illustrative of the gospel message, a true expression of divine compassion, and a definitive verification of His messianic credentials.

But physical healing was neither the central point of His message nor the main purpose of His coming. Again, He came to make propitiation for sin and to purchase redemption for sinners. And He did that by suffering in their place—dying for their sins.

The gospel, then, proclaims the way to forgiveness, redemption, a right standing with God, and the gift of eternal life. The gospel is not a guarantee that earthly suffering will be banished from our experience. It does not promise immediate or automatic healing from every physical affliction. In fact, suffering itself can be a grace by which we are perfected—molded into the perfect likeness of Him who suffered in our place (1 Peter 1:16–17). "To you it has been granted for Christ's sake, not only to believe in Him, but also to suffer for His sake" (Phil. 1:29). And "the sufferings of this present time are not worthy to be compared with the glory that is to be revealed to us" (Rom. 8:18).

The true meaning of the gospel—and its central truth that God is a saving God—is bound up in an accurate understanding of that famous prophecy in Isaiah 61:1–3, which Jesus read aloud in the synagogue in Luke 4:18–19: "The Spirit of the Lord is upon Me, because He anointed Me to preach the gospel to the poor. He has sent Me to proclaim release to the captives, and recovery of sight to the blind, to set free those who are oppressed, to proclaim the favorable year of the Lord." The "poor" whom He promised to bless are "the poor in spirit, for theirs is the kingdom of heaven" (Matt. 5:3). The "captives" to whom He proclaims liberty are "those who through fear of death were subject to slavery all their lives" (Heb. 2:15)— meaning those who are in bondage to sin (Rom. 6:17). The "blind" who recover their sight are those who "turn from darkness to light and from the dominion of Satan to God, that they may receive forgiveness of sins and an inheritance among those who have been sanctified" (Acts 26:18). And the "oppressed" who are set at liberty are those who were formerly under the oppression of sin and Satan (10:38).

In other words, what the gospel announces is something that the physical healings merely symbolized—something more vital, more lasting, more momentous, and more real than temporary relief from the pains of earthly affliction. The gospel gives us the only true, abiding remedy for sin and all its guilt and repercussions.

Furthermore, because we gain so many eternal benefits

from our earthly sufferings, the mercy that sustains us through our suffering is actually a greater mercy than if God were to simply erase every trace of hardship or difficulty from our lives. To put it plainly, instant healing would not be spiritually as valuable to us as the all-sufficient grace that cares for us in the midst of our suffering (2 Cor. 12:9–10). "Therefore we do not lose heart, but though our outer man is decaying, yet our inner man is being renewed day by day. For momentary, light affliction is producing for us an eternal weight of glory far beyond all comparison, while we look not at the things which are seen, but at the things which are not seen; for the things which are seen are temporal, but the things which are not seen are eternal" (4:16–18).

Still, because we know God never changes, we can say with absolute certainty that He is a saving God whose heart is full of compassion for those who suffer. Our lives and ministries should reflect that compassion as well—especially toward those who are burdened with relentless physical agony in this life. We cannot proclaim the love of God faithfully if we neglect that duty.

An Explicit Command for Christians

Our God is a saving God. Lovingkindness defines His character. If we are to be "be imitators of God, as beloved children" (Eph. 5:1), then showing mercy to the weak and infirm is the duty of every believer. "Freely you received, freely give" (Matt. 10:8).

In Luke 14:12–14, Jesus gives us a direct instruction that stands as a mandate not only for the church but for each individual believer. He says, "When you give a luncheon or a dinner, do not invite your friends or your brothers or your relatives or rich neighbors, otherwise they may also invite you in return and that will be your repayment. But when you give a reception, invite the poor, the crippled, the lame, the blind, and you will be blessed, since they do not have the means to repay you; for you will be repaid at the resurrection of the righteous." Could that possibly be more clear? I don't see how.

Jesus is saying that if you are hosting a celebration or a feast, you shouldn't invite only those who can pay you back by giving you a reciprocal invitation. Invite people who have no capacity to pay you back in any way. If you want to manifest the love and compassion of God, that is the way to do it. True Christlike generosity means showing kindness that can never be repaid. When you are lavish in giving to someone you know will be bountiful in return, that is not the generosity of God; that is the typical, shallow altruism of human self-interest. Only when you are generous to those who are powerless to reciprocate are you truly showing the generosity of God. And if you really want to enter into the joy of God, there is no better way.

The church was not established as a country club or a fraternity house for fit, cool, and stylish people. It is a fellowship of those who recognize their own fallenness and utter helplessness, who have laid hold of Christ for salvation, and whose main business on earth is showing other needy sinners the way of salvation. If we neglect to reach out especially to those who are blind, infirm, or otherwise disabled, then we are simply not being faithful heralds of the tender mercy of Christ.

That is a solemn command from Christ. It is a practical mandate that should characterize our relationships with others on a personal level, in the context of our families, and especially in our fellowship with other believers. Let that be the spirit that permeates our dealings with our neighbors, so that Christ might be glorified in all that we do.

NOTES

Chapter One

1 Some material in this chapter has been adapted from John MacArthur, "Who Chose Whom?," Grace to You, Dec. 1, 1997, www.gty.org /resources/sermons/GTY65/who-chose-whom, and from John MacArthur, "Divine Immutability and the Doctrines of Grace," foreword to *Foundations of Grace*, by Steven J. Lawson (Orlando, Fla.: Reformation Trust, 2006).

2 Cited in Arthur Pink, *Studies in the Scriptures,* vol. 9 (July 1938), 218.

Chapter Four

1 Archibald Alexander Hodge, *Outlines of Theology* (New York: Robert Carter and Brothers, 1866), 127–28.

2 Thomas Watson, *A Body of Divinity* (London: Thomas Parkhurst, 1692), 47.

3 R.L. Dabney, *Syllabus and Notes of the Course of Systematic and Polemic Theology* (St. Louis: Presbyterian, 1878), 172–73.

4 Augustine of Hippo, *The City of God*, trans. Marcus Dods (Peabody, Mass.: Hendrickson, 2009), 568.

Chapter Five

1 Bernard of Clairvaux, "Jesus, the Very Thought of Thee."

Chapter Six

1 Some material in this chapter has been adapted from John MacArthur, "So Loved," *Tabletalk*, May 2016, 10–11.

2 *The Works of Robert G. Ingersoll*, 12 vols. (New York: Dresden, 1900), 2:361–62.

SCRIPTURE INDEX

ABOUT THE AUTHOR

Dr. John MacArthur is the pastor-teacher of Grace Community Church in Sun Valley, Calif., as well as an author, conference speaker, president of The Master's College and Seminary, and president and featured teacher with the Grace to You media ministry.

In 1969, after graduating from Talbot Theological Seminary, Dr. MacArthur came to Grace Community Church. The emphasis of his pulpit ministry is the careful study and verse-by-verse exposition of the Bible, with special attention devoted to the historical and grammatical background behind each passage. In 1985, Dr. MacArthur became president of The Master's College (formerly Los Angeles Baptist College), an accredited, four-year liberal arts Christian college in Santa Clarita, Calif. In 1986, he founded The Master's Seminary, a graduate school dedicated to training men for full-time pastoral roles and missionary work.

Founded in 1969, Grace to You is the nonprofit organization responsible for developing, producing, and distributing Dr. MacArthur's books, audio resources, and the *Grace to You* radio and television programs. *Grace to You* radio airs more than a thousand times daily throughout the English-speaking world, reaching major population centers with biblical truth.

It also airs nearly a thousand times daily in Spanish, reaching twenty-three countries across Europe and Latin America.

Since completing his first best-selling book *The Gospel according to Jesus* in 1988, Dr. MacArthur has written nearly four hundred books and study guides, including *Our Sufficiency in Christ, Strange Fire, Ashamed of the Gospel, The Murder of Jesus, A Tale of Two Sons, Twelve Ordinary Men, The Truth War, The Jesus You Can't Ignore, Slave, One Perfect Life*, and the MacArthur New Testament Commentary series. His titles have been translated into more than two dozen languages. *The MacArthur Study Bible*, the cornerstone resource of his ministry, is available in English (NKJV, NASB, and ESV), Spanish, Russian, German, French, Portuguese, Italian, Arabic, and Chinese. In 2015, the MacArthur New Testament Commentary series was completed.

Dr. MacArthur and his wife, Patricia, live in Southern California and have four married children: Matt, Marcy, Mark, and Melinda. They also enjoy the enthusiastic company of their fifteen grandchildren.